About

David Pearl is an innovator in business, the arts and social change. Drawing on a lifetime's experience in opera, theatre and film, he has pioneered the use of the arts in business and is creative confidante to high-profile CEOs and their teams across the globe. Known as the 'Experience Engineer', responsible for designing, orchestrating and animating on and off-line high-stakes meetings, David's work has appeared in media such as the BBC, *The Sunday Times*, *New Statesman*, *The Independent* and *The Telegraph*.

Wanderful is David's third book, following *Will There be Donuts?* (*The Times* Top 10) on the art of meeting and *Story for Leaders*, a handbook for anyone who wants to harness the engaging power of narrative.

David is the founder of the non-profit social venture, Street Wisdom (streetwisdom.org), which transforms ordinary city streets around the world into inspirational learning zones through its free, guided, physical and virtual WalkShops. He keeps his creative instincts sharp by making up operas on the spot with his improvising ensemble, Impropera (impropera.co.uk).

David describes the common thread between all his work as finding the magic in the everyday.

He lives in London and Italy with his family and is an enthusiastic, if out of breath, road cyclist.

Find out more at davidpearl.net and see David sharing at TEDx how he invented the technology behind Street Wisdom on YouTube (bit.ly/2OTJgdn).

What people say about David's other books…

On *Will There Be Donuts?* 'A very rare beast … a highly read-able book about business life that offers road-tested advice and entertaining anecdotes. It will definitely improve your meetings.' *The Times*

On *Story for Leaders* 'The art of storytelling is at the very heart of inspiring others. David Pearl is a master at this.' Ian Buchanan, CIO, Barclays

Wanderful

David Pearl

unbound

This edition first published in 2020

Unbound
6th Floor Mutual House, 70 Conduit Street, London W1S 2GF
www.unbound.com
All rights reserved

ISBN (eBook): 978-1-78965-074-7
ISBN (Paperback): 978-1-78965-073-0

Cover design by Leagas Delaney

Printed and bound in Great Britain by Clays Ltd, Elcograf S.p.A.

Dedication

*'You road I enter upon and look around, I believe you
are not all that is here,
I believe that much unseen is also here'*

Walt Whitman, Song of the Open Road

*To all the teachers I have been lucky enough to meet
along my way. Especially Liz Handy (1940–2018).
You helped me see the unseen.*

Super Patrons

Lorna Prescott

Hugh Riddell

Nik Roberts

Natalie Rossiter

Danny Scheinmann

Chris Sollett

Daniel Stane

Sue Steward

Tim Stockil

Bryony Taylor

Lorraine Taylor

Gregory Thompson

Susannah Tresilian

Anke Verhees

Nicole Verity

Olga Vysotska

Sarah Waite

Karen Ward

Rachel Wiles

Marc Wright

Contents

I Wake to Walk and When I Walk I Dream

I wake to walk and when I walk I dream.
High five leaf! Landing back on my feet,
What the street is, is not what it seems.
All roads lead to the Rome of the heart.
I couldn't curb my enthusiasm for kerbs.
I wake to walk and then I walk my dream.
The word street has the word tree in it!
Someone says God says I'm going to hell.
What the street is, is not what it seems.
You never step in the same street twice.
An old man eats an ice-cream with a flake.
I dream to walk and when I walk, I wake.
Something is hidden in every moment.
Here, a girl is laughing behind a lamppost.
What the street is, is not what it seems.
We are all in the gutter, but some of us
Are looking at it, wondering what it means.
I wake to walk and when I walk I dream.
What the street is, is not what it seems.

Street Wisdom Poet-at-Large, Philip Cowell

1

(Best Foot) Foreword

'I've never been for a walk…'

A young woman has just stood up at the end of a Street Wisdom event we are running for a giant electronics company; she has tears in her eyes. She's one of 250 hard-working store managers who we have invited out of their normal workplace and immersed in a very different environment, one which they wouldn't normally associate with learning – the street. And now, reflecting on her experience, this young woman has something to say.

'I just realised I have never been for a walk…'

You can hear a pin drop, she goes on to explain. She's a doer, constantly busy, on her way from here to there. For her the street isn't a place to dwell, it's just the space between one task and another – something to be got through as quickly as possible. Her Street Wisdom experience has made her realise that she's been marching through life, looking straight ahead, never allowing herself to look around, dawdle, deviate or connect with the world.

She's forgotten how to wander, and looking around that large conference room, I see that she's not alone.

I wrote this book for her, and for the millions of us like her. We hurry through the day, head down, task-oriented, whilst treating the business of getting from A to B as a tactical challenge or as wasteful downtime to be minimised. Moving *forward* seems to be the only way forward. Meandering is fine for holidays but it's not something we can justify on a working day. Reflection is something we'll do when there's time on the agenda – which there rarely is. Indeed, when unexpected pauses do come our way – jams, queues, disruptions, diversion, delays – we fill the time by checking our phones, replying to emails, catching up on the news, replaying in our minds what has just happened and preparing for what's to come.

Like the girl in the seminar, we're stuck in our familiar paths and miss the possibilities hiding in the side roads. We're so focused on getting to our destination, that we can lose our sense of direction on the way. We may look like we're on course, but inside there's often a nagging feeling that we're heading somewhere which we don't want to go – and, at speed.

It's stressful, a challenge to our well-being, and it can be lonely. As Zachary, my teenage son, was explaining to me the other day: 'In an urban setting everyone is on their own. No one is speaking really. If you are by yourself, you are very isolated – headphones on, sunglasses on, hoody up – that is how it is now.'

But is that how it has to be?

This book is an invitation to break the lockstep of modern life and take yourself for a creative meander. It is an invitation to unhook from the devices, switch on your innate navigation system and plot your own distinct course through life. And as you'll discover when you do, there's a reason why wonder and wander are almost the same words.

To be frank, I also wrote this book for me.

As leader of an international social venture bent on getting the world wandering, I had questions I wanted to explore more deeply. How can we be *purposely purposeless* in a world where productivity rules? Why are we so obsessed with straight lines when Nature teaches us to wiggle? What's exciting about being lost and how is it different from feeling lost? How can we read the street as though it's a book full of messages for us? When you come to a crossroads (in life), which way should you turn? Are people we don't know really strangers? And if so, how is it that they can sometimes offer us better advice than people who know us well? If you could set the pace in your life, would you choose the one you are marching to right now? When something wonderful happens 'by chance', what's really happening and can we make it happen more often? And, perhaps most importantly of all, what can spending time on an everyday street teach us about navigating complexity at a time when the world is sorely in need of new direction?

I wrote *Wanderful* to explore questions like these and hope you'll enjoy accompanying me into some fascinating side streets, hidden alleys and secret gardens in search of answers.

David Pearl

London, September 2019

Introduction: New Navigation for New Times

I have deep reservations about the effects of technology on our environment, our societies, our communities, our electoral systems and our world in general. But, if there's one digital advance that gets my like, my five-star rating and heart-shaped favourite sign, it's Satellite Navigation, satnav or GPS if you prefer.

The Pearls don't own a car anymore but when we do travel by road, this navigational gizmo gets us where we want to go – beating traffic, skirting roadworks, alerting us to lurking speed traps and most importantly, pre-empting domestic collisions between my wife and I. Jo has a great sense of direction. I do not. But I am a man, and men, you may have noticed, find it challenging to admit that they don't know where they are. We're just not built that way, which is why the early journeys of our marriage were fraught with huffs, long drawn-out sighs, snapped 'are we there yet?'s and some outright yelling.

Wouldn't it be great if there was a satnav for our lives? A

system we could trust to get us where we need – and, more importantly, want – to go. A methodology that could help us thread our way through complexity, filter the noise and stay orientated – a satnav for the soul.

I think I may have invented one. At least, that's how Street Wisdom is being described.

Candidly, that wasn't my original intention. My first experiments focused on exploring the street as a place to feed our creativity. That's my day job – helping businesses and those who lead them to be more creative. And, it's why I started taking people out of their steel and glass offices – literally out of the box – into the surrounding streets to connect with the world and people outside. But, as Street Wisdom has grown (at the time of writing this, more than 500 events have been staged in over forty countries) more and more people are using it to find and maintain professional and personal orientation.

And not a moment too soon.

NEW TIMES

To borrow a phrase from Madeleine Albright: 'I am an optimist who worries a lot.'

Albright is a real hero of mine. She arrived in the United States as a wartime refugee from Czechoslovakia and rose to be its first ever female Secretary of State. Scholar, teacher, writer, diplomat; she has seen more of the world than most. The fact that she's both encouraged and alarmed by what she now sees resonates with me.

Certainly, when you take a look around there's plenty to be both joyous and fretful about. Every day gives cause for hope and disappointment. Dazzling breakthroughs are offset by frustrating breakdowns. Unparalleled prosperity co-exists with epic inequality.

We're able to peer into the deepest reaches of the cosmos but can be blind to the person right next to us. We've never had more access to knowledge or behaved with such monumental stupidity.

My friend Jim Garrison, former President of the State of the World Forum, puts it this way: 'Things are getting better and better and worse and worse faster and faster.'

We've been here before. In the opening lines of *A Tale of Two Cities* (1859), Charles Dickens famously describes the volatile period before the French Revolution as neither 'the best of times' nor 'the worst of times' but both simultaneously:

> It was the best of times, it was the worst of times, it was the age of wisdom, it was the age of foolishness, it was the epoch of belief, it was the epoch of incredulity, it was the season of Light, it was the season of Darkness, it was the spring of hope, it was the winter of despair, we had everything before us, we had nothing before us, we were all going direct to Heaven, we were all going direct the other way.

I like to think of our times as neither good nor bad, but new. 'New' in that, while much is familiar from previous ages, the diversity, complexity and velocity of what we're experiencing is unprecedented. The options we face are bewildering and the dilemmas and trade-offs increasingly demanding. The choices we make feel ever more significant, but it's like every junction we arrive at has a vast number of possible turns.

It's a paradox. Never before has every inch of the world been mapped out. There's almost nowhere you can get lost any more. And yet, we're collectively disoriented. We're hurrying down a road that has existential consequences for us as a species, with less and less time for course correction. Do we head 'direct to Heaven', as Dickens puts it? Or turn 'the other way'?

That's a question we all have to ask and answer.

There is no shortage of people offering us their guidance.

But they do it, usually for a price, or a vote, and who is to say their 'best way forward' is ours?

Anyone who tells you they *know* what's coming is deluding themselves. We're off the map. And ploughing straight ahead on our customary compass setting is clearly not going to work. These are indeed New Times, and it's high time we found new ways to guide ourselves forward: new paths through the noise, more heart filled, soul driven and wiser.

I think I have found one. I'd like to share it with you, and with as many people as possible.

NEW NAVIGATION

Street Wisdom is a learning experience that uses the streets to help you have new ideas, solve problems and, most importantly, figure out the best way forward for yourself. Instead of relying on technological route-finding, it's a way of switching on your own personal navigation system and steering your own path to the answers you need right now. It's human navigation for a complex world.

Wisdom isn't a word you'd typically associate with the street. Crime, yes. Protest, increasingly. But why wisdom? This approach is based on the idea that there's an inexhaustible supply of ideas around us all the time, if we know how to look. Answers are everywhere, if we reach out and ask. The world is our creative playmate, if we're willing to play. Street Wisdom uses the street and the urban landscape as the stimuli and mirror for our thinking. It awakens our sensibilities and fires up our innate intelligences. So whatever next steps people are contemplating – major or minor, private or work-related, life purpose or lifestyle purchase – Street Wisdom gives them a way to make better, more informed, creative decisions.

For many, particularly those caught up in high velocity careers, Street Wisdom is a chance to get your bearings, and then, intuitively, to prioritise the competing demands on your time.

Instead of sitting and thinking, it invites you to go and have a creative conversation with your surroundings, to stop charging about like you know where you're going, hit the pause button and discover where you *want* to go. This increases your chances of ending up where you want rather than where everyone else wants you to be, whilst feeling better, more confident and prouder of the course you are taking.

It's also an experience that has a way of magnetising you towards the people you need to meet and things you need to learn.

There's nothing 'new' about the elements. Much of what we are doing is reawakening our ancestral senses and skills for use in the contemporary world. But, they are combined in a way that is new, fresh and accessible for the world in which we live.

HOW IT WORKS

At the heart of Street Wisdom, is a three-hour, experiential walking workshop. That's a bit of a mouthful so I came up with the simple name *WalkShop*. It typically involves a group of up to ten people, led by a volunteer facilitator who has been trained remotely using our specially designed online tools. We have also adapted our WalkShop techniques to bring the magic of the street inside our homes. So, when we can't get outside, we can still find everyday inspiration. Every day.

The experience is structured in three parts, each an hour long. In the first phase, participants Tune Up their senses so they connect in a much more accurate way than normal with all that's going on around (as well as within) them. In the second phase, each participant thinks of a question and then goes for a wander through the streets, using their heightened awareness to see what answers they get. We call this phase, with slight tongue in cheek, the Quest, partly because it has a question at its heart but also because it is, in a way, a mini heroic journey. In the final Share phase, the group gathers in a predetermined place (usually a friendly cafe) to discuss what happened during the Quest, what they learned and how they can apply their learnings.

When it's over, people leave with a technique they can use anywhere, any time, to turn on a heightened awareness and connect with the wisdom that's all around.

It sounds simple, and it is. But that's because we've taken many years to simplify it.

I should explain that I spend a lot of my professional life designing and leading extraordinary events around the world. They are usually high stakes, pretty elaborate and very demanding to stage. I wanted these WalkShops to be so uncomplicated that anyone could lead or take part in one, in any street, anywhere in the world. An everyday wonder – every day.

Once we had made it really simple, we gave it away. That is to say, inspired by the open source and shareware movement, we made the instructions available to the public for free. The thousands of people who have experienced Street Wisdom so far have done so without any charge. The social movement is funded by donations and, increasingly, the for-profit projects we create for businesses around the world.

We encouraged volunteers to run events and supported them when they did. In return we asked that people share stories of what they are experiencing out there in the streets – and they have, in their hundreds. This book is informed by all they've been discovering.

Quickly, the events became a movement. I know everyone is using the m-word currently, but I think Street Wisdom's growth can justify it being called at least a mini-movement, especially because getting out into the world and *moving* is what it's all about.

Today, participants are finding Street Wisdom a powerful way to activate their awareness and log into the database of latent wisdom that surrounds us. At a time when we're increasingly lost in our heads, disorientated by fake news, closed-loop networks and bias-reinforcing echo chambers, Street Wisdom helps us to turn our attention outwards again – to escape the mental musing and daydreams and enjoy a present tense, right-here-right-now, full-sensory life experience of being human.

Augmented reality is a new buzzword, beloved of technologists who are keen to plug us into machines that make everyday reality 'more interesting'. I think of Street Wisdom as throwing a switch so we can experience reality as the multidimensional wonder that it already is, without strapping on a plastic headset.

For an approach that's all about way-finding, it can seem strangely disorientating at first. But that's intentional because it asks you to dial down the reasonable, know-it-all, agenda-setting part of your mind and have an adventure instead. The uncertainty we feel when we really start mentally off-roading is just the know-it-all part of our minds struggling not to learn something new. Sometimes we have to get lost to find what we're looking for.

Importantly, Street Wisdom is designed to work in the towns and cities where, increasingly, more people live. Ours is going to be an urban century, where we live together in concentrated and hopefully more sustainable ways. The planet can't afford for it to be anything else. Street Wisdom is a way of bringing those places to life. It reminds us that inspiration doesn't have to be a fuel-guzzling plane flight away. We don't have to – and shouldn't – wait until holidays for reflection time. Enchanting though Nature might be, there's just as much wonder on the street outside, once we know how to find it.

We realise, that for too many people the streets are currently anything but an inspiring setting; they can be unsettling places. Thinking more positively about this resource of ours – and yes, most streets legally do belong to us, the public – is key to the movement.

WANDERING THROUGH *WANDERFUL*

Because wandering is something to experience, I have structured this book less like a read and more like a stroll. If you haven't already experienced one of our WalkShops, I am hoping this will convey something of the joy and magic of sauntering through a town, being stimulated, puzzled, awed and delighted by what we see and who we meet. If you *are* already familiar with Street Wisdom, then I am hoping this book deepens your understanding of what's going on beneath the surface, and sharpens your curiosity to seek further.

I should say now, this book is *not* a how-to manual for Street Wisdom (if you want the detail on how to experience and/or run a WalkShop feel free to head to streetwisdom.org), nor is it a Street Wisdom promotion. I don't want to 'sell' these ideas to anyone. Use them if you like, but feel no pressure. Street Wisdom is about the opposite of pressure. When I refer to our Street Wisdom events, mechanism, history, participants and people, it's because our experimental social venture has generated much of the book's content. This is more of a stroll through the ideas *behind* Street Wisdom – its intellectual, philosophical, historical, scientific and spiritual backstreets, if you like – and it's going to be a voyage of discovery for me as well.

SO WHAT LIES AHEAD?

I have written the book in three phases, which loosely follow the profile of a Street Wisdom event – preparation, wandering and reflection. That said, the chapters are self-contained, so if (like me) you're allergic to reading a book cover to cover, you are very welcome to dip in and out as you wish.

It's easier to find your way forward once you know where you are. In *The Road to Here* I share the backstory of Street Wisdom, plotting some of the highs and lows from my own life that brought me – and this is still something of a surprise to me – to be leading a plucky, international social venture that's fast wandering its way around the globe. The next thing we need to do is awaken our senses, which means activating our many intelligences, not just our mental reasoning. As we'll explore in *Tuning In,* those intelligences reside throughout our bodies, not just in our heads. Which is why getting out into the streets and beyond the limits of brain logic makes real sense. As Fleur, a client of mine put it recently: 'Street Wisdom is a way of making your unconscious, hidden thoughts visible in the streets around you – a way to find out what you're thinking'. This chapter explains how.

Extraordinary things regularly happen on Street Wisdom events: wildly improbable coincidences, unlikely things discovered precisely when they are needed, the right people popping up just when they should.

In *Synchroni-City* I take a look at what's really going on, with the help of Carl Jung, shamanism and an onion. Is this happening to us? Or are we making it happen? What are we doing to make the world co-operate better with us and how can we do this more reliably? I am saying this before we set out so you can decide how much wonder you are prepared to let into your daily life.

Now we saunter through a sequence of six chapters, each of

which explores an aspect of the Street Wisdom experience and what we can learn there about how to live, work and navigate life more wanderfully.

If we're going to wander and be truly purposefully purposeless, we are going to have to break out of the tyranny of straight-line thinking and reset our course *Off the Straight and Narrow.* When we're tuned in, we find the urban environment is constantly sending us messages, stimulus, and answers to our questions. As one Street Wisdom participant beautifully put it, the city is a *Stone Book,* but it's one that we have to learn to read, decoding its signs, signposts and symbols. Time for a *Change of Pace.* We often bemoan the speed of city life but velocity itself isn't the problem. Yes, slowing down enriches many facets of life but lots of things are better faster too. The key is to reclaim control of your own personal tempo. We'll also explore what it means to get *Lost and Found* and we'll take a look at why we resist losing our way, but why that's often essential – mentally, creatively, spiritually – to find what we're looking for.

We won't be alone on our literary amble. There will be many others out there on the street with us – people we don't know and would probably, under normal circumstances, avoid. Here we cross the space that divides us from them and learn about the *Wisdom of Strangers.* You're actually going to be bumping into strangers throughout this book, as you might in a real city, because between each of the chapters you're going to be invited to *Meet A Stranger.* These are all people I have met on my own journey and each have their wisdom to share. They're brilliant folk and many are quite well known but you'll notice I only use their first names so you can meet them authentically, as fellow wanderers, rather as you would a stranger on a street. If you're interested to know who they are and more about their considerable achievements, you'll find a gallery of their portraits and biographies at the end of the book *(Meet the Strangers).* I should also mention here that I often refer to Street Wisdom participants and the experiences they have had. Mostly I have used real names but occasionally, where appropriate, have disguised identities.

Just before our wander finishes, we'll find ourselves at a *Fork in the Road*. Navigation is all about making choices, responding to conditions and making course corrections as we go. Now it's decision time and we'll explore how the street can help you make better, richer choices for the way ahead.

We'll bring the book to a close, as we do in Street Wisdom, by considering what we've learned on the way and how we can use this in the future. We'll gather in the *Connection Cafe* to share some thoughts and end – appropriately for a walking experience – by looking at the next steps you and we might like to make.

THANK YOU

Before we begin, I'd just like to thank you for buying and now reading this book. Street Wisdom is a non-profit organisation that offers its public work free around the world. Our mission is to bring inspiration to every street on Earth. When you consider how difficult life is on many of those streets, this is not a small challenge. But that's the galvanising power of a mission, right? All proceeds we receive from sales are donated directly to our social venture. So, by purchasing this copy, you've already helped make this world just a little more wanderful. On behalf of the whole Street Wisdom team, thank you.

3

The Road to Here

*'People usually consider walking on water or in thin air a miracle. But
I think the real miracle is not to walk either on water or in thin air,
but to walk on earth. Every day we are engaged in a miracle which we
don't even recognize.'*
Thich Nhat Hanh

**The system in this book is the outcome of many years'
researching, exploring and tripping over unexpected
insights. Before we set off wandering, let's understand
where we've been and how we got here.**

So here we are, standing on the street. We could be on any
street, anywhere in the world. But I have chosen one in London's Covent Garden. It's spring of 2013. The first ever Street
Wisdom event is about to begin, and it's raining.

We're about to set off into a book about how we better orientate ourselves in a complex world. I expect you're keen to
plunge straight in but it's hard to know where we're going if

you don't know where we've been. So let's first backtrack in time so I can share some key moments in the Street Wisdom journey and highlight a few of the life-changing experiences that nudged me into inventing it.

A word before we do: it's going to get wandery. The story is going to slip and slide from place to place and time to time. But that's how life is. It makes sense now, with 20:20 hindsight, but at the time I had little idea where this unfolding story was leading me.

Ready for a bit of geographical and chronological wandering? Great.

Back we go to 2013 and let's take a look at the street where we find ourselves. There are six streets actually, all converging on a small, cobbled roundabout where we're standing. Welcome to Seven Dials. The seventh 'dial' is the obelisk behind us, completing the sundial feel.

Don't mind the rain. We city dwellers get all hunched up and grouchy when it rains. Just think of it as Nature's way of reminding us she exists, even in the city. Also, as my mother used to say to us as kids, 'you won't melt'.

Covent Garden used to be London's main fruit and vegetable market. Though there's no sign of a garden now, back in the 1500s that's exactly what you'd have seen here: a high-walled convent garden that produced the vegetables for Westminster Abbey.

Covent Garden is the setting for the opening scene of Shaw's *Pygmalion* and of *My Fair Lady*, the film of the play. It's also home to the Royal Opera House, an imposing, ivory-coloured temple of passions and prima donnas where the young me had one of those life-changing experiences I just mentioned. The stage door, where the artists enter, is all steel and glass now. But, back in 1970 it was old brick and peeling green paint, and yes, that wide-eyed nine-year-old is me, being led through the doors and along a rabbit warren of corridors and up to the stage by my school teacher, Pat (who discovered I had a singing voice) and my vocal coach, Jean (who knocked it into shape). The stage is all hustle and bustle with scene shifters, stage crew and chorus members. Above, is a criss-crossing mesh of lights and ropes, to my left the achingly vast auditorium and directly in front of me, the conductor. It's Puccini's opera *Tosca*. The third act opens on a Roman dawn with the song of a local shepherd boy. That's my role. And this is my first ever rehearsal on stage. It's terrifying but I make it through and feel a hand patting my shoulder. 'Bravo' whispers a T-shirted, Latin-looking, young man beside me. Then he walks on stage, opens his mouth and sings. Plácido Domingo went on to become one of the world's greatest opera tenors but at this time he was pretty well unknown in Britain. So, the exquisite, golden sound rolling out of his throat stunned us all. It was the most intense, and yes, magical, thing I had ever experienced, and it reset my expectations of life. This was my new 'real'. Something inside me said, if this is possible, I want more – every day.

I didn't know it then but the pursuit of everyday magic was to become a red thread through the ups and downs of my life.

I did go on to sing opera as an adult – still do. But I wasn't going to be a full-time opera pro. I didn't quite have that golden throat and baulked at the incredible focus and single-mindedness that life as a top singer requires. When seductive and creative byways opened up, I was just too curious to say 'no'. So I played double bass in orchestras, studied English (not music) at university, wrote in film and advertising, set up an opera-cum-circus company, studied improvisation, presented music shows on the BBC and through that fell into working with businesses, helping organisations and those that lead them be more inspired and inspiring.

The Covent Garden of my youth is long gone, transformed

from a working food market to a trendy shopping and tourism destination – all fashion brands, craft stalls and high-end espresso. The area has been truly scrubbed up and the rotting cabbage leaves I remember being stuck to the cobbles are long gone. It's normally awash with visitors, but on the day of Street Wisdom's debut, the drizzle kept the tourists away.

Let's swing up Neal's Yard and turn left down Monmouth Street. See that big, damp Union Jack flag hanging over that portico? It's the Covent Garden Hotel, once a Victorian hospital. Across the road, the full-on erotica at Agent Provocateur seems out of place until you remember Covent Garden was also at one time London's red-light district.

We've arrived at the meeting point. And waiting for us are two friends of mine. Confusingly, they are both called Chris. One has a clipboard and the other a big smile.

Chris Baréz-Brown is the one with the grin. You may know his name from his life-enhancing books like *Shine*, *Free!* and *Wake Up!* Chris is something of a genius at bringing positive energy to businesses all over the world (through his consultancy Upping Your Elvis). And when it comes to new creative ideas, he's what you might call an early adopter.

When I told him about my early experiments with creative wandering (over several mojitos), Chris immediately saw its potential as a way for us 'to rediscover ourselves'. Chris's enthusiasm is infectious, which is why he's not only here himself but he's invited a gaggle of mates and clients to join us. They will be here soon.

Over there is Chris Sollett, a long-time friend and ally from my other life in theatre and a natural wanderer himself. But today he's here to stage-manage and oversee what's about to happen, hence the clipboard.

Standing there in London's drizzly theatreland, the curtain is about to rise on the Street Wisdom story.

Strictly speaking, I should say this is Street Wisdom's *public* debut. In private, I had been playing with street-based learning for years. Back in 2010, I'd run a programme (with friend and collaborator Darius Norell) called the Invisible University on these very streets. It was quite an elaborate affair. Clients showed up and were split into groups, each of whom spent an immersive morning with a guide, someone who saw the streets (and life) through an unusual filter. Guides included an ex-SAS soldier, an artist, a medic, a busker and a martial arts sensei. Participants spent the afternoon experiencing the street from the fresh perspective they'd explored in the morning. While they walked, we asked participants to consider a question they wanted to answer and to see what stimulus the urban environment offered them.

But it was too elaborate, and simplification takes work.

To refine the concept, I ran a series of experimental street-based workshops in Amsterdam with my friend and ally Peter Merry, and we christened them WalkShops. At the time, Peter was the head of the European arm of Wisdom University, a non-residential graduate school for those wanting to explore spiritual and philosophical studies in a rigorous, academically accredited way. It was in a conversation with Peter that I first used the phrase 'street wisdom' to describe the experience. It pinged, and stuck.

Back in Covent Garden, the Chrisses and I are looking at the drizzle and wondering if the weather is going to be a problem. We needn't have worried. Over the next few years we were going to discover that some of the best Street Wisdom events are held in driving rain, and the participants barely seem to notice. In fact, so-called bad weather adds to the adventure.

But while a lot of experimentation took place in London and Amsterdam, the inspiration came from Italy. More precisely, it was handed to me on a note, handwritten by an Oracle. It's nearly 10 a.m. and the Street Wisdom participants are beginning to arrive. But there's time to explain this mysterious statement.

To do so, we'll have to time-travel to 2001 and relocate ourselves to the Piedmont, the foothills of the Italian Alps.

Head south-west out of the medieval town of Ivrea, waving as you pass through Castellamonte (home of the 'stufa', Piedmont's iconic ceramic stove), and dogleg up into the mountains. Climb the winding, dwindling road and eventually you'll come to the hamlet of Baldissero Canavese. Keep going another two-thirds of a kilometre. Then stop. You've arrived at Damanhur, an eco-community-cum-living-experiment-cum-research-centre-cum-spiritual-hub unlike any other.

It's the closest thing to a real Hogwarts I have ever experienced. Except here the magic is real and practical. This remarkable and intentional community has its own currency, education system (UNESCO recognised), fire department, complementary health service, food production, organic wineries and a host of other retail businesses. It has a government called the Game of Life, a sacred wood, a labyrinth, a complex, mosaic-encrusted underground cathedral known as the Temples of Humankind, celebrating not one but all religions, and, that Oracle I just mentioned.

The Oracle is not a person, more a kind of spiritual advisory service for when you're pondering questions, particularly the bigger questions in life. You feed in a question, wait a few months while the Oracle team do some research and then, under a starry sky and full moon, you get handed your *risposta* or answer. Mine was a couple of pages long, written in a beautiful calligraphic hand. The language was poetic, coded language, designed to make you reflect. Years later, I still return to it and reflect more. But one phrase immediately popped out at me at the time. It roughly translates as, 'walk in circles in public places'.

I was intrigued but mystified. What could it mean? I returned to the city and – did nothing with it. I shoved this nugget of spiritual wisdom to the sock drawer of my mind, where it lay unused for years. Then, in 2005, feeling creatively stumped, out of road and needy of inspiration, the phrase popped back into my mind.

'Walk in circles in public places.'

With a bit of distance from the magical mountainside, I decided not to ponder but to take the instructions literally. I took a bus into the centre of London, chose the busiest place I could find – Leicester Square – and started walking in circles.

I can't pretend I was comfortable starting. Going round in circles is pretty much the textbook definition of futility. I was sure people would think I was crazy. So I cheated a little at the start, walking such a big circle right around the outside of the square that no one could track my lunatic behaviour. But as I got bolder, I tightened the circle until I was more or less turning around myself. Despite my fear, no one seemed to notice me. I was effectively invisible.

I was rediscovering something that the flâneurs of nineteenth-century Paris had already discovered (we will meet them later too): a crowd is the perfect place to disappear.

I found this anonymity incredibly freeing. Apparently unobserved, I could really observe those around me. And in many of their eyes I saw a look that reminded me of when I was growing up in the opera world. We called it 'snake eyes'. The tenor would appear to be gazing lovingly at the soprano, but actually he was staring inward, worrying about the next high note. His eyes would take on a glassy, veiled, somewhat reptilian look. Next time you are in a busy street, take a look at your fellow pedestrians. Are their eyes looking outward, curiously scanning what's around them, or inward, focusing on where they've been and where they are hurrying to next?

Heeding the oracular advice and circling Leicester Square helped me realise the street is an extraordinary place to play. It's not just a convenience, a way of getting from A to B. It can be a potent creative playground.

So far, the journey has taken place in Britain, Holland and Italy: vegetables and oranges, opera and oracles. That's the backstory almost told. Almost. But to fully understand the genesis of Street Wisdom, you need to know it started with a bang. Not the Big Bang, though it had a universe-shaking impact on me. But a bang, nevertheless. Or, to be more precise, it started with the scream of car tyres and then a bang.

It was 1969 and I was walking to school with my little brother. Neither of us saw the stolen car coming. It missed me, but caught Jonathan, and things were never quite the same. I'll spare you the grisly details because my intention here isn't to shock you. It's more to share what shocked me. And started me wandering.

Let me quickly say that Jonathan (my brother) fully recovered. He's a successful lawyer and happy family man with some dashing scars he still likes to show off. But my own relationship with reality never quite fitted back together. In a few seconds I can still see them playing behind my eyes as the solid, predictable world was thrown into the air, and, once the horror had worn off, I found myself thinking: reality isn't as real as the adults have been telling us.

Reality being unfixed was scary, yes, but also something else. Because if a great day can turn into a nightmarish one in a split second, isn't the opposite also true? Awful could turn into marvellous in the blink of an eye. It felt to me like the extraordinary lurks at the edges of the ordinary. Just when you think life is predictable, it isn't. Routine is a breath away from drama. Accidents can happen. But, so can miracles.

And talking of miracles…

If we'd had to wait for an ambulance to arrive, it's likely Jon would have died. Fortunately, luckily, miraculously and ever so implausibly, a decorated ex-solider happened to be walking down that very street at just the right time. While the other passers-by looked on in horror, he realised the urgency of the situation and looked for a way of transporting Jon to hospital immediately.

Second miracle: another ex-serviceman was delivering wine to an off-licence in the street. They gently transferred my brother into the back of the wine van and got him to hospital, a fifteen-minute drive away, in eight minutes, almost certainly saving his life.

And that heroic stranger's name was – Mr Chance. Fortuitous in both name and nature.

Luck? A random occurrence? Happenstance? That's what the rationalist within me wants to believe. But my experiences that day and my researches ever since point to a deeper connection between apparently random events. With Street Wisdom, I wanted to explore a way of encouraging more happy accidents, more reliably, into our lives. And you'll discover more about how to do that later in the book.

I wish the incident hadn't happened. So does Jon. But looking back, it was the first and most dramatic piece of street wisdom I've ever received.

For now, the rain has stopped. And the participants for our first Street Wisdom are gathering. Let's join them and prepare for a truly magical wander together.

EXERCISE: YOUR WANDERFUL LIFE

What?

An exercise to remind us all we've been wandering since birth.

Why?

When I ask clients around the world to describe their road to here, they usually give me a list of events and achievements. A then B then C, and so on. Nothing wrong with this sequence of facts. But it's boring – A CV. Indeed, if this were a real road to here (and that's actually what curriculum vitae means – road of life), it would be dead straight and dull. Also, it's not even half of the story. Our lives rarely go to plan. Like all good stories, they zigzag between highs and lows. And it's when things don't go to plan that we learn the most. As I think you'll agree about two minutes from now.

How?

As a warm-up for the proper exercise, in the next sixty seconds I would like you to describe your road to here, connecting the key events and moments with the words *then… then… then.* You can do this with a partner, or simply record yourself on your smartphone, keeping your eye on the clock.

Great.

Now I'd like you to describe the same journey but using different connector words: BUT then… SO then. *but then… so then…*

Here's mine. In sixty seconds. With no punctuation.

I was born in the rural suburbs *BUT* my parents wanted me

24

and my three siblings to have more educational choices *SO* they downsized and moved us to the heart of London I was an average eight-year-old *BUT* with abnormal musicality and a loud if rough voice *SO* my teacher arranged an audition at the Royal Opera House where I discovered the intensity of emotion and that was going to be my life *BUT* my voice broke *SO* I took up playing the double bass (unexpected I know!) and toured the world with orchestras *BUT* I come from a Jewish background where the arts are seen as risky *SO* I went to Cambridge and fell in love with literature thank you Mike and Laurette *BUT* was not cut out for academia *SO* came seriously unstuck seriously profoundly life-threateningly unstuck – the wandering route by definition has its ups and downs – *BUT* the darkness I have learned as I have crashed about is part of wholeness *SO* I started therapy and writing for advertising in the day and singing opera at night I loved opera *BUT* it was too conventional *SO* when I went by chance to see a circus – Archaos – I thought these two art forms could be combined and co-founded Opera Circus which toured the world and *that* was going to be my life *BUT* one day some curious business people saw me presenting a music series on BBC and asked me to talk to them about how the arts could 'help them connect with each other in ways they wouldn't have dreamed possible' was this a deviation or a synthesis of two of my great interests human development and creativity? there's only one way to find out *SO* I opened an experiential events company with my friends *BUT* eventually disbanded it *SO* I started another and found myself designing and leading all sorts of wonderful elaborate experiences for organisations around the world – I call it Experience Engineering *BUT* began to notice that people would return from these enchanting retreats to offices where nothing had changed *SO* I started taking people out of their offices into the streets to discover that extraordinary experiences are available everywhere right on your doorstep *BUT* I wanted to include people outside business *SO* I invented Street Wisdom…

OK. A little more than sixty seconds. But this is my book and I can bend the rules.

Now it's your turn. Your road to here in sixty using BUT then and SO then. Deep breath and bon voyage…

Then look back at those two tellings and consider, the word that forces them to be so different is 'but'. When we admit the 'buts' in our lives, we are telling people that our lives didn't go as planned. And what do you call people whose lives don't go to plan? That's right. Humans.

Whether we realise it or not, we're constantly wandering, and it's an important part of what makes us human.

You can see a digital version of this exercise here: streetwisdom.org/wanderful-exercises/

You're just as likely to bump into Patrycja on a street in Sydney, New York or Warsaw. As it happens, today she's walking in London's Fitzrovia and she doesn't have much time. Fortunately, Patrycja is a human who is comfortable with velocity. I once asked her how she read so many books and she explained she listens to audio books at double their normal speed. 'The human ability to learn is absolutely amazing,' she explains, 'and I don't think we give ourselves enough credit about how much information we can soak up and how fast.'

But then knowing about how the mind works is Pati's job. 'Self-Hacking' as she calls it, is a powerful weaving of psychology and neuroscience that's seriously in demand by organisations and their leaders all around the world.

You sense her mind is whirring, but you wouldn't know it to look at her, completely happy browsing central London in the September mini-heatwave. As we chat idly, I realise that browsing is something she's had practice at.

She says, 'One of my advisers called me intellectually promiscuous. I prefer to think of myself as sapiosexual, attracted to people's minds as much as their bodies. I love having conversations with people who have a completely different view, a perspective I know nothing about. I think of it as getting lost in the streets of intellect and ending up in different neighbourhoods of your mind.'

Is that a metaphor or does the mind really have neighbourhoods?

'Yes, we have neighbourhoods,' she replies, the scientist kicking in. 'But they are woven into one big city, bigger than the sum of its parts. Researchers keep looking to find which region of the mind does what and then discover that other areas can take over if needed. Like a city. Interdependent.'

We've stopped by some graffiti art, beautifully drawn in spare, chalk lines on a boarded-up shop front. Is there a neighbourhood in her mind dedicated to art... a neural cultural quarter?

'I think that my art is immersing in the neighbourhoods and then finding my way back to understand the map. I am sure you know Alfred Korzybski...'

Not only do I not know him, but I couldn't pronounce his name. But let's keep that to ourselves. Especially as he is, according to Patrycja, 'one of the smartest guys of the twentieth century'. Embarrassing. 'He's the semantics pioneer who said that, "the map is not the territory". I think that's brilliant. A map can tell us about the layout of this area, but to know how it looks and feels, I have to come here and explore.'

And explore she has! Patrycja explained that she left home in Poland when she was sixteen and then lived on four continents.

What's the secret of being comfortable with so much travel and movement?

'The first thing I did when I came to a new place was to go on the street and ask myself, "Do I look like a person from here?" I would immerse myself in the city not just watching people but mimicking how they walked and talked – their speed, particularly. I found I can fit into other people's tempos pretty easily, and that's really important. The research shows that when you attune to another person, your rhythms sync up. Which, I think is quite lovely. It's quite remarkable how you can become a different person, become the city in this way. To me, since I was a kid, that has seemed like magic. In the city you can be whoever the hell you want. You can be by nature quite shy, but you can say, today I will be an extrovert, and you start switching the map.'

Many of Patrycja's clients are people who might describe themselves as pretty rational and want to 'hack' themselves so they can think in different ways. For Patrycja, there's a key right here.

'If you want to be more creative, immerse yourself in another culture and become that culture. The most creative people I know do this. Look at the great writers in the twentieth century. They wouldn't

29

just be visiting Morocco or Afghanistan or Cuba, they'd be living there – immersing themselves. Today, I think we travel more but we arrive less.'

And talking of arrival...

We're getting close to the time of Patrycja's business call – an important one – but we're not as close to her hotel as we thought. We've taken the wandering seriously. So she switches on Google to help direct the conclusion of our wander together.

'Human subconscious is like a NASA supercomputer, while the conscious mind is more like a Post-it note. My strategy, including at work, is to dump everything we know into the supercomputer, mix it up, steer it in a direction and see what emerges. It's like wandering in the streets. My colleagues have been asking, "do we have the framework", and I have had to say, "I'm sorry, we don't". But it will emerge. In fact, something is emerging right now. Not just in my mind, in theirs. You need to be analytical, of course, but also patient with the emergence. Like having two lungs to breathe with.'

It's been a very satisfying wander. And we've arrived at the zebra crossing outside her hotel – with a little help from Google – just at the right time. As Patrycja strolls over the pedestrian crossing, she points to the smartphone app and laughs.

'The map is not the territory but sometimes it will help get you where you want to go, right?'

30

4

Tuning In

'The body knows everything. We know very little.'
Fritz Perls

**If we are simply going for a walk, our rational brain is
sufficient to guide us. But to access the full, inspirational
power of wandering, we have to awaken all of our
intelligences, not only in the head but throughout our body.**

It's February 1882 and a young electrical engineer is strolling
through a city park in Budapest. He is enjoying the late afternoon, reciting stanzas from Goethe's *Faust* to a friend. Suddenly he freezes and starts frantically drawing circles and wavy
lines in the dirt with his walking stick. The engineer is Nikola
Tesla, and the world-changing breakthrough he is animatedly
describing to his friend is an iron motor, spinning rapidly
in a rotating magnetic field produced by the interaction of
two alternating currents. A few years later, the AC induction

motor, patented by Tesla, quickly becomes the electrical work-horse of the modern age.

It just goes to show, breakthroughs can happen any time, anywhere – whilst slipping into a warm bath, watching an apple fall in an orchard or out walking in a city park, like Tesla. But most of us are not Tesla, nor Archimedes nor, for that matter, Isaac Newton. And, for most of us, flashes of inspiration seem both random and rare. In developing Street Wisdom, I wanted to find a way we could all summon breakthrough ideas for ourselves more reliably and more often.

After years of experimenting, I devised a simple method to do this. We call it the Tune-Up. The name owes something to my musical background and the idea that before we play, we need to prepare our instruments. But more importantly, it reflects a conviction that the inspiration we are seeking is all around us and that all we need to do is tune in to that abundant field of stimulus to find what we are looking for.

The Tune-Up is designed to do that. It's a series of short walks, each with a simple instruction you follow while you walk. Every instruction activates a different way of perceiving and connecting with your surroundings. When you experience these four walks in cumulative sequence, the effect on your awareness can be quite profound. Even life-changing.

I could share them with you now and we could head straight off on our wander. I have a hunch your brain would prefer to get on with it. But that's the everyday brain, the one we use to navigate from task to task, home to workplace and back, and that brain is likely to get in the way of a truly wonderful wander. So, before we get into some serious sauntering, I am going to suggest we pause and explore why that is.

WANDERING ISN'T WALKING

To be clear, wandering isn't walking.

Walking is movement with purpose. From time to time, Street Wisdom events coincide with official walking tours, and the difference between us is immediately obvious. The walkers are on a mission – to retrace the footsteps of a great painter, maybe, see twelve churches in three hours, or visit the sites of famous murders, hangings and hauntings. Here they come, striding through, usually in the wake of a mega-phoned guide with a brightly coloured feather on a stick. They have hats and eye-shades, binoculars and cameras. Several carry those ergonomically designed walking poles – probably essential when you are scaling a Nordic mountain but of questionable use on a pan-flat city pavement, and their rugged outdoor clothing is festooned with enough zips to make a punk rocker swoon.

We love the walkers, but they're all about purpose – collecting information, better understanding the location, learning history or seeing the agreed 'sights'.

Wandering has a purpose too, but it's to be purpose*less*. If purposeful purposelessness sounds confusing, there's a good reason. That's because, at this phase of our development, humans are obsessed with being productive.

PRODUCTIVITIS

Productivity is actually a relatively new concept for humankind. We first see the word in the 1700s. That's because our species spent its first couple of hundred thousand years on Earth surviving: hunting, gathering and, later, farming. The idea of productivity is associated with generating over and above what we need to keep the wolf from the door. It's the key to wealth and thence leisure – to capitalism itself, with all that it brings.

An early adopter of productivity was the prodigiously talented and incessantly industrious statesman, author, scientist, inventor, activist, diplomat, amateur architect and all-round polymath, Benjamin Franklin. This founding father of the United States would rise at 5 a.m. and divide his days into neat time boxes, each with an assigned task:

> Rise
> Wash and address Powerful Goodness[1]
> Contrive day's business and take the resolution of the day
> Prosecute the present study
> and Breakfast.

All of that *before* breakfast. Exhausting. But this productive schema clearly worked for Ben Franklin. We have him to thank for the world's first political cartoon, the lightning rod, bifocal spectacles, the development of demographics and not to mention the US Declaration of Independence. But his tick-box approach to time management has also helped spawn the modern To Do list, endless self-help books on how to wring the absolute most out of our working day and a nagging sense that if we're not being productive, we're wasting our time.

Ben Franklin's regimen includes another clue to why productivity attracts us. Every day began with the morning question, 'What good shall I do this day?', and concluded with a review of whether and to what extent the day's ambition to Do Good had been realised. This twinning of productivity and virtue took hold. Productivity came to be seen as making you

---

1. This is Franklin's delightfully oblique way of saying 'Pray to God'.

richer, more fulfilled, more effective and also a better person. No wonder it has taken over our lives, even outside work.

I took up road cycling a few years ago as an antidote to an intense, three-in-one career where I was working business, arts and social change all at the same time. I loved the fresh air, the conversation and the coffee. For me, cycling is the unavoidable, sweaty bit between one espresso and the next. I was attracted by the low-key, amateur, take-things-at-your-own-speed spirit of the sport. I scoffed at the city girls and boys who swooshed past me, heads down, eyes glued to their bike computers, heartbeat readouts and performance scores. I mocked them for turning their sport into a job, for treating each ride as a tick on a training schedule. Then I bought a bike computer and, of course, became just as obsessed.

And here's one problem with an apparently purposeless activity like wandering. Time has become our currency, a resource to be spent well. If we are not investing time in productive activity, we are 'wasting' it – not only inefficient but morally wrong. That leads to a working culture where stress is constant, burnout frequent and something as apparently aimless as wandering seems delinquent, like 'bunking off', as British schoolchildren describe missing lessons without permission.

We see this when we run Street Wisdom for businesses. For organisations that have become used to the idea that working *hard* is working *well,* stepping out of the glass and concrete work space seems like playing hooky – that is, until participants discover that there's more inspiration in the average street than the average office.

But time management and morality are not the only reason we resist the lure of aimlessness. Being purposeful is hardwired into our brains.

BETWEEN PAVEMENT AND CHIN...

Let's take a look at the brain for a moment. There it sits on the top of the body, like a CEO installed in a penthouse board-room, its high opinion of itself confirmed by having pole position in our physical real estate, and by centuries of flattery from philosophers and religious thinkers.

The brain is excellent at some things – analysis, processing and recalling information, calculations, language, spreadsheets and sudoku, but ask it to wander and it'll tell you 'wandering is beneath me'. It's absolutely right, only not in the way it thinks.

For below the brain, occupying the space between the pavement and the chin, is the body. The relationship between the mind and the body goes way back, but it hasn't been an easy one. And for the last couple of thousand years, the body has been very much a junior partner.

It all started well enough. Mind and body collaborated pretty well together in prehistory. Early humans had little time to philosophise about where body ended and mind began. Day and night, they were focused on the business of hunting, gathering, picking juicy nits out of their hairy bodies and generally staying one step ahead of extinction.

Progress and civilisation brought with it the revolutionary boon of 'spare time' – for the lucky few, at least. Leisure, the absence of physical striving, quickly became an aspiration, a marker of achievement. It still is.

We revere the ancient Egyptians for their monumental achievements but they were evidently quite 'a sluggish and sedentary people'. Or so Bruce Chatwin describes them in his book *The Songlines*. He also points out that their evolved mythology of afterlife was a mental compensation for physical immobility, a way to 'project on to the next world the journeys they failed to make in this one'.

Many of the ancient Greeks (those who weren't slaves, that is) spent their time thinking, or as they called it, philosophising. I picture them lolling around in their tunics, eating peeled grapes and noticing that their minds could be fizzing with ideas while their bodies were idle. And if the mind could operate without the body – they must be separate, right?

Initially, the Greeks saw mental and physical as equal partners, the one feeding the other as complementary parts of the well-rounded human. Plato, no slouch in the brain department, used to proudly claim that he was also an accomplished wrestler. But Greece's early thinkers and athletes soon separated into separate camps. When planning his educational system, Aristotle warned that students would have to choose between mental or physical training in the same year, 'since the two kinds of exercise naturally counteract one another, exertion of the body being an impediment to the intellect'.

From then onward, things only got worse for the body.

The earliest Christians showed growing contempt for all things physical. Despite the miraculous account of God breathing life into dust (Genesis 2:1), the body came to be seen as the antithesis of heavenly – an earthly trap for all things bad. St Paul was a prominent voice in the anti-body movement, deeply suspicious of what he called 'sin's instrument'. St Francis of Assisi, normally quite a compassionate chap, mockingly referred to his body as 'Brother Ass', a churlish slap in the face for both bodies and donkeys.

The body was seen as a rogue beast that had to be controlled. The most common methods were to starve it, deprive it of sleep and then whip it (literally, with a lash) into subservience. St Dominic would apparently beat himself three times a night: once for his own sins, once for the sins of the world and once for the sins of those in purgatory. Masochistic? Certainly. But nothing if not methodical.

Christians weren't alone in their campaign against all things physical. Most world religions, including Hinduism, Buddhism and Judaism, show varying amounts of suspicion for the body's wants and needs.

The strained relationship between body and mind underwent a full-blown divorce in the seventeenth century. When René Descartes stood up and declared 'je pense donc je suis',[2] he inaugurated a dualistic world view that split matter from mind and put thinking (and by this he meant rational thinking) at the centre of our very being. Reasoning became the source and *only* proof of our identity.

The Age of Reason had many beneficiaries. The body was not one of them. It was consigned to second-class citizen status, bowing and tipping its forelock to the noble brain. And it has remained in that subservient position into our own times.

I recently came across a copy of Rodin's *Le Penseur* in a gallery. There he was, surrounded by lively statues of dancers, spear throwers, dragon slayers and frolicking lovers, seated solidly on his backside, straining. The message is clear. Thinking is something you do sitting down. Mental activity is the antithesis of physical.

How often have I heard 'serious' types in businesses around the world gravely say, 'We have to sit down and sort this out?' Sitting is actually the last thing they should do. It's not only unhealthy, but also unproductive. 'Sitting is the smoking of our

---

2. Translated into Latin as it duly was, cogito, ergo sum ('I think, therefore I am') had the ring of universal truth – one that leaves no room for doubt. Indeed, doubt is just another thought and therefore another proof of the principle or, as Descartes put it: 'We cannot doubt our existence while we doubt.' Checkmate, any non-believers!

age', says the Harvard Business Review[3], but the association between immobility and thinking is a strong one to break.

Physicians, psychologists and psychiatrists have all recently developed much more holistic views, taking a more 'whole person' approach to health and well-being. Yet, in my experience, people still think of the brain as where thinking is done and the body as its transport system. The truth, as scientists are now discovering, is very different.

THE THINKING BODY

In the 1980s the Harvard psychologist, Howard Gardner, famously listed seven types of Intelligence: Visual–Spatial (good at visualising), Linguistic-Verbal (uses words well), Interpersonal (understanding and interacting with others), Intrapersonal (self–awareness), Logical-Mathematical (good at analysing problems), Musical (good at thinking in rhythm and sound) and Bodily-Kinaesthetic (physical movement). More recently he's added Naturalistic (relating to/in tune with Nature), with a possible ninth – existentialist intelligence. Critics challenge whether these are intelligences or talents or characteristics, but it's hard for either side to prove as there is no universally accepted definition of intelligence. Researching this book, I found over fifty. Whatever your view, one thing is becoming clear: our intelligence – or rather our complex, interlocking set of intelligences – does not reside exclusively in our heads.

In his book *Intelligence in the Flesh*, the eminent psychologist Guy Claxton traces the rise of what cognitive scientists now recognise as embodied intelligence. This is the growing under-

3. https://bit.ly/37znqVi

standing that, while reasoning may be performed in the head, thinking happens throughout the body:

'My mind was not parachuted in to save and supervise some otherwise helpless concoction of dumb meat,' says Claxton. 'No, it's just the other way round: my intelligent flesh has evolved, as part of its intelligence strategies and capacities that I think of as my "mind". I am smart precisely because I am a body. I don't own it or inhabit it. From it I arise.'

So no longer does everything revolve around the brain in its bony penthouse on top of our spines. This is a Copernican revolution in how we think about how we think.

Andy Clark, Professor of Logic and Metaphysics at the University of Edinburgh, describes the profound shift in this way:

'Gone is the central executive in the brain – the boss who organises and integrates the activities of multiple special-purpose subsystems. And gone is the neat boundary between the thinker (the bodiless intellectual engine) and the thinker's world. In place of this comforting image we confront a vision of mind ... not limited by the tenuous envelope of skin and skull.'

Based on my experiences at Street Wisdom, I'd agree. Not only does our intelligence fully occupy our body, it exceeds the body too. It's as though we have an extra-physical brain, that can reach out, beyond our physical limits, and interact with our environment.

But don't take my word for it.

Let me share the four tune-up exercises we've devised to awaken your embodied intelligence and you can go experiment for yourself.

TUNE-UP #1: AWAKEN YOUR BODY'S COMPASS

We want to awaken the intuitive guidance system within us that's always sending us prompts but is not always heeded. So, the first instruction we give to participants is:

Be drawn to what attracts you – and notice what doesn't.

The idea is that you go for a short solo mini wander (of about ten minutes), keeping this instruction in mind and see what happens.

Why this instruction first? Because it encourages curiosity. It reminds people that their environment, however urban, is full of attractive detail if you really look. It also encourages movement. It asks participants to physically move towards whatever attracts them. We did this as children, remember?

Wherever you are reading this book, pause for a moment and take a look around. How is it that you know what everything you see tastes like? The doorknob, wallpaper, leaf, tree bark, iron railing, shop window… It's because as children we put everything in our mouths! Taste is one of the most powerful ways we learn, discern and make preferences. And we'd physically follow those preferences. When we were three years old, if we saw a cake or a toy we'd have made a beeline straight for it, but education and culture have subdued that spontaneity and physical demonstrativeness out of us (put the cake *down*, *don't* barge in front of the queue, no touching without *permission*). At Street Wisdom we want to free up our bodies physically to carry us (and our brains on top of us) towards and away from what does and does not attract us. This proves very useful later in the process when you use the street to help you choose between competing options, or help you find the new direction you really want to be travelling.

GASTRIC NAVIGATION

Listening to your body's intuition is often called 'following your gut'. And it turns out there are sound, biological reasons for this.

In a world where the brain is king, the gut is relegated to the level of a food and sewerage operation. However, there's lots of evidence that the gut, specifically the intestines, not only do quite a lot of thinking for us but actually predate the brain.

Every creature on Earth is constrained by its energy budget; the calories obtained from food will stretch only so far. Brains are metabolically expensive – drawing thirstily on the body's available energy reserves. Our early hominid ancestors would have struggled to consume enough calories from raw food to support much in the way of mental activity. Anthropologists now think changing our diet – and specifically our harnessing of fire for cooking – was the key to creating enough surplus energy to develop the prefrontal cortex, the folded, neurally rich area of the brain where much of our advanced thinking is done. Preheating, grinding and chopping food outsourced a lot of the effort of getting calories into our bodies and we reinvested this energy into creating a brain. To the truism 'we are what we eat', we should add 'we are who we are because of how we learned how to eat'.

So the brain owes its existence to the gut. And its primordial influence on our thinking continues to this day. The vagus nerve, the longest nerve in the body, wanders[4] its way from the gut to the brain, controlling swallowing, speaking and bearing vital information to the brain about the state of the body's organs. Yes, *to* the brain. Ninety per cent of the nerve impulse

4. Vagus actually means wandering in Latin.

traffic is one way. Which means the head, despite its physical superiority, is actually taking a good deal of its instructions from down below.

The gut may affect our conscious thinking even more profoundly because at the microbial level our gut isn't really *ours*. We humans are inhabited by trillions of bacteria, viruses, parasites and fungi. Most of us, by cell count, belongs to these microscopic colonists. Seen that way, each of us are only about 43 per cent human[5]. The largest and most complex microbiome is housed in our intestines, home to trillions of bacteria. Each of these has its own life cycle and evolutionary agenda. Our own genome – the code that makes us human – comprises about 20,000 instructions or genes. Add all the genes in our microbiome together and that number balloons to a dizzying 20 million. Essentially 'we' are two genomes. The human and the microbial that augments our own – and affects it.

A non-human example shows just how powerfully microbial flora and fauna can influence a host's behaviour. Meet *Toxoplasma gondii*, the parasite that causes toxoplasmosis. This resourceful little microbe can only reproduce in the guts of cats. But to get there it first infects mice and, sitting in the rodent's intestines, switches off the gene in the mouse's brain that makes it fear cat odour. The newly rewired mouse, with parasite on board, now fearlessly strolls up to the next kitty and – hey presto – *Toxoplasma gondii* has an express, first-class ticket to its ideal reproduction grounds in the cat's tummy.

Scientists are now exploring how gut microbes can control human DNA[6], switching our genes on and off to suit their plans. We don't yet know how profoundly microscopic stow-

5. https://www.bbc.in/2AICIAD
6. Geneticists are now exploring how gut microbes can influence human DNA: https://bit.ly/30Lf8bv and https://go.nature.com/2AF6elh

aways within us are influencing our own behaviour but even the possibility reinforces the importance of whole-body awareness when you are making your way through life.

A QUESTION OF JUDGEMENT

Before we move on to the second tune-up, I just want to draw your attention to the second half of this initial instruction. Noticing what *doesn't attract* us helps us become aware of the myriad judgements (usually unconscious) we are using every day to filter what we experience.

As we walk down a street, we are assessing which strangers are safe and which a threat; we're estimating where it's OK to linger and where we should hurry on; we're evaluating what and who is and is not to our taste.

There's nothing wrong with filtering the tidal wave of information we receive every moment. If we didn't, we'd drown in data. But helpful as judgement is, it also constrains our thinking, our creativity and ultimately our freedom.[7] Working, like many legal systems do, on the principle of precedent, we judge the present by what's happened before. If not checked, our future route through life is directed by what has worked and not worked in the past. In this way, judgement is anathema to creativity, reducing the terrain of our imagination and keeping us trapped on an ever-reducing island of our own 'rightness'.

The idea of this tune-up, and of Street Wisdom generally, is to disrupt the routine thinking process, to encourage participants to explore byways they haven't in the past, open doors they wouldn't normally, meet strangers they would typ-

7. It's what psychologists call Reproductive rather than Productive thinking

ically avoid and generally entertain intriguing possibilities they would typically walk straight past.

TUNE-UP #2: PRESS THE PAUSE BUTTON

You can read more about this later (see *A Change of Pace*, page 151) but an essential part of the preparation for wandering is to slow right down, or as we say in Street Wisdom tune-up:

Slow (pause for breath)

Right (longer pause for breath)

Down (longest pause for breath)

We've learned to really accentuate the point – to draw out the instruction – because though the meaning is clear, the brain doesn't really 'get it' at first. The productivitis-infected brain wants to get this task done and move on to the next. To get the benefit of this tune-up, we have to go slower than the brain wants us to. And that means slowing the body first. So keep walking but do this as slowly as you can without actually falling over. It's interesting to discover that a body – like a bicycle – is actually hard to balance at very slow speed. And that forward motion is one of the things that keeps us stable. Maybe that's why we hare about such a lot.

When you blink, blink slowly. When you turn your head or move your arms, do that slowly. Like you were walking through viscous liquid.

If you're thinking that it might be uncomfortable moon-walking down a city street, you'd be right. And that's also part of the tune-up, recognising how we often go at the city's crazy speed for fear of standing out, looking odd, attracting attention. But having the courage to set your own pace, to march to the beat of your own drum, is an essential part of freeing yourself to really wander. Effectively, by dictating your own tempo, you're reclaiming sovereignty of your time and, for the duration of the wander, your life. Again, we'll dwell more on this in the *Change of Pace* chapter.

Crucially, when you breathe (and it's good to keep breathing), lengthen the gap between your in- and out-breath. The depth and cadence of our breathing has a profound effect on our mental state. That is the reason conscious breathing techniques like pranayama are at the heart of meditation practice. As the Buddhist philosopher Thich Nhat Hanh puts it, 'breath is the bridge which connects life to consciousness, which unites your body to your thoughts. Whenever your mind becomes scattered, use your breath as the means to take hold of your mind again.' There are sound physiological reasons for this, explains my friend Jaime Lee – surgeon turned management consultant and now head of the Australia-based wellness company Health Quotient:

'From a physiological perspective, when your body perceives an acute threat, the reptilian part of our brain "hijacks" the rational and logical part of our brain and all thought processes bypass the neocortex. Hence during such an acutely stressful event it is almost impossible to think clearly and act rationally. However, through using your breath you can override the hijack. On the inhale, you increase the oxygen to your brain. On the pause, you slow down. On a slow exhale (double the time of the inhale), you are telling your brain that you are safe. Then the "hijack" will pass and there you will be to face the situation with more clarity and calm.'

Breath is also the most direct link between the outside world and our interior. It's no accident the word 'inspiration' means 'to breathe in'. How we breathe directly affects our ability to process what we are experiencing. It can be the key determinant in whether that experience is positive or the opposite. As Fritz Perls, the father of Gestalt therapy, put it: 'Anxiety is excitement without breathing.'

It may take a while, but slowing your body down has a profound effect on your awareness, with participants often telling us they hear more, see more, notice details more.

People often describe our work as urban mindfulness. I am delighted to be associated with a movement that is making such a helpful impact on modern life. That said, I'd like to point out that what I feel is a subtle but important difference. In my view, mindfulness teachers often want us to still our wandering minds whereas I feel Street Wisdom encourages the mind to go for a wander and see where it takes us!

Breathing certainly helps bring your mind into the present moment. And that's important because your mind spends most of its time either remembering the past or speculating about the future. This incessant rewind/fast-forward activity accounts for a lot of our mental chatter. Your body's senses, however, operate in the present, alert to what's happening NOW. As Fritz Perls liked to exhort his patients: 'Lose your mind and come to your senses.'

As you 'get present' to all that's happening around you, reciprocally you find yourself noticing your inner experience – the thoughts, feelings and impulses that are constantly flowing within us. We carry within us a wealth of wisdom. An experience like Street Wisdom helps us connect with that as much as the wisdom outside and around us. I like to think that the discoveries we make in the street are just reflections of what we are discovering within. But that's for another chapter.

TUNE-UP #3: SWITCH ON YOUR MEANING MAKER

The rational mind has been somewhat on hold for the past two tune-ups, and that was intentional. But we can feel it straining at the leash, wanting to get involved, and if we don't give it something constructive to do, it will distract us and find something it prefers. Fortunately, there is something our minds can do marvellously well and which is super helpful for inspired wandering: to see patterns between disparate things, to join the dots and to make meaning.

The Gestalt Movement, which shook psychology when it emerged in Germany in the 1920s, claimed our ability to see patterns in the world around us – to grasp that the sum is greater than its parts – was central to our cognition. Even intelligence traditionalists, like the people who put together the basic IQ (Intelligence Quotient) tests, say pattern recognition is a key determinant in a person's potential to think logically, verbally, numerically and spatially. Business psychologists also tell us the ability to spot existing or emerging patterns is one of, if not *the* most critical skill in decision-making. Having a superb pattern detector and creator on board is going to be a huge asset, especially when we get on to the next phase – the Quest – where we ask the street a question and need to decode the signs, symbols, sounds and other stimuli that the street sends back in response.

So in this tune-up we ask participants *to enjoy, discover, decode and/or follow the Pattern(s)*. The precise wording varies depending on what the event leader intuits each participant will most respond to. But the intention is the same in all cases: to exercise our mental meaning-making muscle and to let this miraculous, uniquely human capacity stretch its legs – literally.

Participants return having found patterns in every aspect of their street experience – sights, sounds, smells – and with a heightened sense of the connection between previously unconnected elements. Participants seem particularly attuned to patterns that are spatial (invisible lines of energy criss-crossing open spaces), sequential (how moment *a* flows meaningfully into moment *b* and *c)* and aesthetic (the pleasing and intriguing effect that follows when you sense how a previously jumbled picture fits together). And so, beauty is where we head next.

TUNE-UP #4: ENGAGE THE POWER OF APPRECIATION

Brain, gut, lungs, feet, arms, ears, nose, eyes… The tune-up is awakening the body, organ by organ, sense by sense. The final instruction is designed to activate one of the most potent direction seekers of all, the human heart.

Like the gut, the heart is an organ with its share of neurons. And, like the gut, it is an organ that communicates with the brain not least to adjust heart rate to work rate. That said, the communication is autonomic and while it's attractive to imagine the heart thinks by itself, it's probably unlikely. If it does, it's certainly not rational. Witness the average teenager in love.

But this instruction isn't just intended to awaken the heart's navigational qualities, to get us following our heart, as it were. The purpose of asking you to 'see [and sense] the beauty in everything [and everyone]' is to awaken that most potent of qualities – unconditional love.

We encourage people not just to see but to sense beauty.

That's because many things do not look, on the surface, beautiful. However, if you sense beneath appearance, beneath those limiting judgements, you can always find at least a grain, a sliver of beauty. I've personally experienced participants who returned from this tune-up wreathed in smiles, having found the beauty in trash (someone's cleaning our town up), cigarette butts (that's a few cigarettes that don't need to be smoked), dog mess (healthy digestion in action) and a flapping piece of black plastic (too long to explain here but basically divine).

Also, though we say 'everything', we include 'everyone'. Again, we are practising melting away the incessant judgements that label strangers as 'ugly' or 'attractive' in a warm wash of appreciation for the fellow human beings we are sharing this street with at this unique, unrepeatable moment. With this attitude, others are beautiful not because they could feature on a *Vogue* cover, but because they are right here, right now, and couldn't be any other way.

Another way of describing the unconditional love this tune-up generates is – appreciation, in its truest sense, which is 'to value' or 'give value to'. It's my conviction that when we love our surroundings, our environment, our society and our planet loves us back.

To bring our stroll through this conversation to a close, I'd like to share a moment of appreciation that helped inspire me to create Street Wisdom in the first place. Join me, if you will, on the top deck of a red London bus, stuck in traffic, at quarter to six on a wintry evening in a pretty ordinary road near my home called Kentish Town High Road.[8] It's more than ten years ago, and it's snowing.

If you squeeze in next to me – and you'll have to, because the bus is packed full of people – and you step into my brain, you'll hear me complaining, 'I don't want to be here,' folded awkwardly into the bus, unable to sit down. My back is hurting. The people around me, frankly, smell of sweat. They pong. Well, take a sniff. Admit it, they do. There's a dog yapping, a baby crying and the bus is going nowhere.

'I don't want to be here!' Not sure if I say that in my head or out loud.

And then something odd happens. Another voice in my head – and it really does sound like another voice – says:

'OK, David. Imagine you are dead.'

Sorry?

'I said, imagine you are dead. Kaput. Obliterated. Consigned to the Eternal dark. Are you doing that?'

I am.

'OK, now imagine you were given the chance to come back to life for sixty seconds.'

Uh-huh?

'Would you take that sixty seconds?'

Of course, I would. A chance to be re-embodied and have another sixty seconds of life? Who wouldn't?

'But there's a condition,' says the voice. 'You have to take those sixty seconds right *here*. Right *now*. Would you still be complaining about the bus, the time, the sweat? Would you still want not to be here?'

---

8. I recently saw a film set in Dickensian London. Charles Dickens actually lived just up the hill in Highgate. At one point the heroine's horse-drawn carriage gets stuck in heavy traffic. She asks the driver the name of the congested area. 'Kentish Town, ma'am.' Clearly this bottleneck has been annoying travellers since Victorian times.

There's a long pause, while the implications of the question sink in. It's the silence you hear in your head when an insight truly lands.

I had to confess to myself that no, I wouldn't be complaining. Imagining myself into those sixty precious seconds, I would be enjoying having a body to be aching. I wouldn't be judging my fellow passengers, I'd be marvelling at their variety, appreciating their fashion choices, savouring their personal perfume. I'd really listen to the squalling baby, the song of infancy. And as the second hand swept around for the very final time, I'd juice every detail for its marvellous, magical, wonderful *now*ness.

I've never forgotten that experience and the lesson it taught me: that we only complain because we think we will live for ever. If we really understood that our time here is limited and of uncertain length, we'd appreciate every moment we had. However much our minds like to speculate on better places we might be, here is where we are. So love the moment.

Insight needs practice to become a daily reality. I think I created Street Wisdom as a way for me to practise getting out of my head, into my body and connecting with all the wonder that's around us every moment. Now let's go practise together.

EXERCISE: FRESH EYES

What?

You can use any of the tune-ups I have described in the previous chapter to help awaken your senses and receive richer information from the street environment. You'll find they make any journey down any street more interesting, and entertaining – even streets you think you know well. Below are some additional exercises specifically designed to help you see familiar surroundings with fresh eyes.

Why?

Many of us – the lucky ones – use our eyes as a principal way of understanding the world around us. We're an increasingly visual age, preferring pictures to text, emojis to explanations. But there's a trap here. Our vision is just as selective as our other senses. There's a lot more out there than meets the eye.

If we want to see the world differently, we have to exercise different ways of seeing the world.

How?

Here are three simple methods to help you really *see*, not just look.

1. A Different Angle

In an early TED talk, the designer Philippe Starck[9] pointed out how the angle of our gaze mirrors our angle of thinking. Concentrate on your feet and it's hard to think more than a few steps (or days) ahead. Shift your gaze too high in the heavens and you can get lost in airy future speculations – and crash into the furniture. He recommends looking just above the horizon, up and over the edge of what you can see, as the 'angle of intelligence'. Give it a try. Notice how you think differently when you drop your eyeline to the floor. Then scan the horizon. Look to the heavens. Peer into the middle distance. Notice how your thinking changes as you alter your eyeline.

2. Side vision

A great theatre director I have worked with, David Glass,

often sits in rehearsals at right angles to the stage and watches the action out of the corner of his eye. It's a bit disconcerting for the performers (if people aren't looking straight at us, we want to know why!) but he does it because you can spot things in your peripheral vision that you miss when you are staring straight at them. It works really well out in the street too. As you're walking, see if you can shift your attention from what's directly ahead and concentrate instead at the very edge of your vision.

3. Defocus

Like a good photographer, your eyes are constantly working to stay focused on whatever you are looking at (near or far) and deliver a sharp image to your retina. It's very helpful but can make life a bit predictable. Try deliberately defocusing your eyes for a change. You can do this by concentrating your gaze on something close (your thumb, for example) while simultaneously staring into the distance. The world suddenly looks more impressionistic, as if you were seeing the world through the eyes of a painter like Monet. You're less aware of detail, but more of form, tone and colour.

You can see a digital version of this exercise here streetwisdom.org/wanderful-exercises/

It's one of those picture-perfect London autumn days you see in the movies: a blue, cloudless sky, crisp sunshine, wheeling pigeons, black taxis and red double-deckers – even flapping Union Jacks and Big Ben. The works.

I'm crossing Parliament Square, and I'm late.

The grand-sounding Peers' Entrance to the House of Lords in London is actually quite a modest black-painted hut – a shed, really. And when I get there, Andrew is already waiting for me.

He's smiling, but looking at my recorder dubiously. 'I am not sure I can be authentic when someone is recording me,' he confesses. Authenticity is, as we shall discover, an important topic for Andrew at the moment, but strolling together past the statues of Churchill and Mandela towards St James's Park, we soon fall into a companionable walking-talking rhythm and the technology is forgotten.

I don't know what you imagine a British Lord looks and acts like, but I'll bet Andrew doesn't fit your stereotype. He's the opposite of pompous – animated, laughing, arms continuously gesticulating, words torrenting out as fast as he can think them but still, low-key. Andrew has no interest in standing out from the crowd. He's much happier immersed among people, taking in all that's going on.

'That's the only way I could do what I did at M&S,' he explains. He left school at fifteen, an undiagnosed dyslexic with no qualification, and rose to be the managing director, running the billion-pound company in his idiosyncratic way. 'I'd wander around the stores, visit the manufacturers, tour all the offices. I'd take in what people were wearing, eating, saying, how fast they walked, the atmosphere, the light and then when a decision had to be made, I didn't tend to focus on the issue in a rational way. Instead, I would become the 14 million customers, the 300 stores, the 36,000 staff and suppliers and somehow or other the answer would come.'

Andrew is miming a meandering zigzag with his hand to show

56

how his mind finds its way. 'I cannot understand things if they are set out in a linear, logical way. I can only understand when I look from all different angles. Dyslexia is part of this. It makes the mind work more holistically.

'The most important thing to me is – mutual respect.' Andrew is well known for his peace-building work in areas like the Middle East and I think this is where the conversation is heading - but he's actually talking about his own creative process, about the different parts of his brain respecting each other.

'There is one part of my brain that is trying to work out how to do things. It's working on a problem, trying, trying, trying to sort it out. The other part of my brain isn't interested. It's just playing with possible futures – quantum, probabilistic stuff. Normally the two sides hate each other and don't talk. However, if you're lucky, and you relax, one starts to look at the other with affection. The player is playing with answers that the worker is looking for.

'Now in M&S, thank goodness we worked like that. I had the highest regard and respect for the people who could do the legal, finance, back office. I knew they could do what I couldn't. And in return, though quite a few of them thought I was a bit annoying and I wave my hands around a lot and sometimes talk rubbish, they'd ask me into meetings because I'd come up with answers they wouldn't have thought of. I'd be doodling and half listening to something on European logistics and... the answer would just squirt out. That's why I want those parts of my mind to have mutual respect.'

Mutual respect isn't exactly a hallmark of modern politics and Andrew is no fan of our polarised, political culture. He doesn't even like the win-lose banter of sports. He's the peer most likely to step into a heated debate with a positive, conflict-resolving provocation. 'I'll be the one saying, "Look, we're not going to get anywhere in the Middle East if Palestinians and Israelis hate each other."' This conciliatory impulse was behind him helping to set up the Mindfulness All-Party Parliamentary Group. 'One hundred and fifty Lords and MPs have done an eight-week course on mindfulness. Now it's physical and we've started a similar group for Yoga. We should have mindfulness in the UN.'

For someone with such an unusual career, it's hard to imagine Andrew being stuck but that's what he was recently told – by his own children.

'Last year I was seventy-five [he doesn't look it!]] and my children said they wanted a serious conversation with me. "You're seventy-five," they said. "You're going to die soon and we're a bit worried you've never appeared on this planet as yourself. Not only does no one else know you, we don't know you. And you don't know yourself. Give yourself a year off. You've been working since you were fifteen... you've done enough."'

Andrew listened and began a new journey – a quest for authenticity. 'I sold my flat and decided "I will not come to the House. I won't jump in to say yes to things and I won't gabble."' Andrew's reticence didn't work as well as he expected. 'I'd keep my mouth shut during meetings and say as little as possible. But the less I said, the more wise people thought I was and the invitations just increased.'

So off to a two-week intensive in vipassana, silent meditation. 'I have meditated at 4 a.m. every day for the last thirty years. But this was nine hours a day, really serious. Five days in, the Abbot called me to his room. "You came here wanting to find the authentic you," he said. "I notice you've changed but there's something I need to point out. Now you are walking, breathing, eating like a monk. If you're not careful you will go back to the world saying you've found the authentic you and it's just another mask!"'

He's been on a course in the Highlands to explore the Tibetan Book of Living and Dying. And spent time with a young PhD who specialises in self-narrative. 'She made the point that we are the stories we tell about ourselves. The truth is, we're not a continuous identity. We actually only live now, now, now, now.'

Coincidentally, his children have made a new request. 'Before you die, we want you to record the hundred stories of your life. No one can tell them like you.' Andrew loves that idea. 'If I do that, I feel I can put all that in the past, and then I can do and be anything I want.'

We've stopped and are meditatively enjoying the flower beds. 'When I do find a new place with a garden and have stopped working and resigned from all these things and I am meditating, cooking and eating...' He trails off as a fresh thought makes him laugh. 'You know what's funny? I keep telling people I am going to go away and they reply, "Andrew, you want to learn how to be the 'authentic you' around people, and you're going to learn this by living in a cave?"' Andrew sees the funny side.

Our own journey is wending back towards the Palace of Westminster. I follow Andrew on to a tourist-packed bridge and he stops, mesmerised. While the tourists are clicking selfies on their smartphones, Andrew is looking at the ducks – really looking. 'See how they are evenly spread. How do they know how to be between two to three yards from each other?' Before I can answer, his attention is on the London Eye, which rises majestically above the park skyline.

'See that wheel? British Airways make more money on that than on their flights. I was looking at it the other day from Hampstead Heath. You can see it from all over London. You know Hokusai and his hundred views of Mount Fuji? What if we got a hundred photographers – just think of how many great photographers there are in this city – to shoot the Eye from different places and put the images in a book? You've got a beautiful product to sell on site or on an app.'

Andrew's wandering produces another idea by seeing the same thing from different angles. No wonder, when Marks & Spencer's chairman, Lord Sieff, came across the young Andrew working in an obscure part of the company, he decided to take him on as his personal assistant, changing his life in the process.

'I probably won't do it,' he adds. 'But I can't help myself from thinking like that.'

On the way back, Andrew spots a family looking for the House of Lords on their tourist map. Ever the supporter, he offers to help with directions. The family smile back but shake their heads and return to their map. Clearly, they'd rather figure it out themselves. I can't help feeling that's a shame. It would have made a great holiday story: being shown to the House of Lords by – a Lord. But Andrew's not fazed, doesn't miss a beat and walks on, smiling.

Then it strikes me. Sometimes it's fun to be lost, and there can be real joy in finding your own way, just like Andrew.

5

___

Synchroni-City

'Synchronicity is when the universe gets personal.'
Robert Moss, Sidewalk Oracles

**The more we wander, the more we seem to experience
strange coincidences and chance encounters. These
apparently unexplainable phenomena are signs that
synchronicity is at work, and that we are connected to the
world and each other far more intimately than we realised.**

Fancy meeting you here. You picking up this book at this precise point in your life and me having written it at this moment
in mine. Of all the books in all the world – I mean, what are
the chances?

OK, it could just be random. You just reached out and this
book just fell into your hand. But what if it's more than that?

Scouring participant accounts of Street Wisdom WalkShops,
it's un-ignorable. People tune up, ask a question and odd stuff
starts to happen. Long-lost friends run into each other by

chance, unexpected objects are found just where and when they are needed, advice is given or overheard precisely when it is most relevant, unlikely revelations, unpredictable happenings, serendipitous bumping...

Something is going on.

Christians might call it grace; Buddhists and Hindus will tell you it's karma; astrologers understand it as the product of planetary alignment; reasonable 'grown-ups' just stare at you with the look of scepticism that says 'really?'.

Yes, really!

In the five or so years since we started Street Wisdom, we've had consistent feedback that out on the streets the daily rate at which 'odd' coincidences occur is somehow increased. More right things seem to happen in the right place at the right time. It's as if someone has tinkered with the default probability filter to allow more fluke and happenstance into our lives. It feels like the world is co-operating with us in a different way, like normal streets become charged zones of possibility, not just delivery systems for commuters. I know the word 'magic' has been somewhat diluted in our digitised, Disneyfied age, but participants have the distinct sensation that genuine magic is afoot.

I confess the idea of creating more magic in our lives personally appeals to me. But this isn't about my view of the world. The beauty of a movement that's so widespread is that I don't know most of the people running or participating in Street Wisdom events. I can't influence a complete stranger in Buenos Aires, Verona, Lagos or Cape Town, and I certainly can't skew their feedback.

Something is *definitely* going on.

The Swiss psychiatrist and psychologist Carl Jung had an unquenchable curiosity about dimensions of existence that are beyond the scope of conventional understanding. These 'paranormal' enthusiasms included telekinesis (moving objects with

his mind), numerology, alchemy, UFOs and predictive dreaming, all phenomena that less open-minded colleagues would
dismiss as hokum. In the early 1900s he became fascinated with
the improbable – in his words, 'acausal' – events that he and his
patients would often experience, coincidences that didn't seem
to have an obvious cause but couldn't be explained as purely
random either. Seeking to legitimise the concept with his scientific peers, he came up with a technical term to describe this
phenomenon – Synchronicity[1] – or, as he put it, 'a meaningful coincidence of two or more events, where something other
than the probability of chance is involved'.

It's the *other than probability* bit that has intrigued and baffled
thinkers from Plato and Spinoza onward. At the heart of the
conundrum is the tension between the objectively knowable
and subjectively experienced aspects of life. If 'synchronicity is
real,' say the objectivists, 'then prove it.' '*Ah,*' respond the sub-
jectivists, 'but mystery doesn't do maths: meaningful coincidences can't be studied statistically.' Interestingly, Jung worked
alongside a scientist, the quantum physicist Wolfgang Pauli,
to shape the concept of synchronicity. In trying to explain
synchronicity, Pauli described the wafer-thin line they were
treading as 'between a blue fog of mysticism and … a sterile
rationalism,' saying that, 'this will always be full of pitfalls and
one can fall down on both sides.'

It's worth mentioning that Pauli was treading his own personal tightrope too: cool, calculating scientist by day, wild
partying womaniser by night. He was also something of a one-
man synchronicity zone. Apparently, machines would break
down whenever he was around.

Working together to articulate synchronicity, Jung and
Pauli felt they had found a missing link between the apparently

1. Jung actually credited Schopenhauer as being the 'godfather' of the idea.

disparate dimensions of matter and mind, a way for our thoughts about the world to affect what manifest in the world. I say 'apparently disparate', because Jung rejected the dualistic idea that matter and mind are made of different stuff, instead preferring to think of all reality as being connected in a single, integrated whole – an *unus mundus*. We'll talk more about that connected view of the world a little later in our stroll but, for now, I want to share a piece of advice a wise friend, the uber-coach Michael Breen, once gave me for when encountering something new, intriguing but apparently unexplainable: 'Don't spend time wondering if it's true. Imagine it's all made up (because it is) and just focus on whether it's useful.'

We could spend the rest of the chapter – and another book or two – trying to figure out whether synchronicity is real or not. And the chances are we'd still not reach a single 'right' answer. There *is* something wonderfully mysterious here. That's probably the point. Mystery wakes us up. It reminds us that all is not what it seems and what we see is not all there is. An insight that arrives in our lives in a way that cannot be explained often has a resonance and significance that means we're more likely to take notice of it.

There might be very good scientific reasons that what we want to know cannot be known. In his famous Uncertainty Principle, Heisenberg proved that, at the microscopic level, you can only be sure of a particle's speed or position – not both. As one of my early co-experimenters Peter Merry, Chief Innovation Officer at Ubiquity University, puts it: 'Cause and effect don't really exist at the quantum level. There is no certainty.'

So what I'd rather do for the rest of this chapter is let go of the need to be right. Let's just accept synchronicity exists for now and focus on how you access its power.

Imagine if you could have that chance encounter more often, summon the unpredictable into your life more predictably, encourage more delightful surprises, feel like the world is working with (not against) you more regularly, access a world of possibility we sense is there, but can only rarely grasp?

There's no one way to do that. Drawing on my own experience and digesting five years of data from Street Wisdom, it's clear there are many access codes to the 'Synchronicity Operating System'. Here, I'd like to share seven and invite you to try them out to find which best suits you. They are all practical – things you can do anywhere, any time without needing any special preparation or the use of drugs (unless that's how you roll).

To explore them, you might want to picture us walking through a covered shopping street browsing the different options. Personally, I see an Arcade of Synchronicity festooned with those twinkly end-of-the-pier lights and full of intriguing store fronts. Stretching before us are seven hanging signs, each with a topic painted on. They read: Imagining, Interpreting, Noticing, Playing, Synchronising, Recognising and Intending. There might be an eighth in the shadows at the end, but we'll come to that. The arcade is inhabited by characters who each have an enlightening take on synchronicity. They're people I've met during my own wanderings and I think you'll find they pop up just when we need them.

You'll notice the approaches we encounter each require progressively more commitment from us. The early ones are really techniques, the later are more ways to approach life.

So, invite your inner sceptic (the party-pooper aspect of the mind that is determined to pick apart any mystery) to go have a short snooze on the bench over there. And let's browse.

1. IMAGINING

Let's make this the first stop in the Arcade because one of the easiest, and most common, ways Street Wisdom participants have found to access a world of meaningful coincidences is simply to use their imagination.

Imagining is such a common human activity we forget how unique and, well, bizarre it is. The ability to make pictures in your mind (the literal meaning of imagine is 'to picture to oneself'), rather than see what is there, is an altered state of consciousness. And we can do it at the click of a finger. Just keep reading these words and simultaneously imagine a pool of water or a desert landscape or a dismantled watch, made of cheese, plus the sound of thunder and the smell of household bleach. Bizarre, right?

The musician and hyper-creative Brian Eno describes imagining as, 'possibly the central human trick', distinguishing us from all other creatures and allowing us to create empathy with others. 'We can imagine worlds that do not exist. That makes us able to experience empathy – having the feeling of what the world is like in someone else's head.' Seeing children playing imagined worlds into being is, in his view, watching them 'become human'.

Having spent a lot of my life creating wildly different experiences for audiences and clients, I have come to think of an experience in its simplest terms as *a time and place where the normal rules don't apply*. That's something we've all been able to do since we were kids. Remember those playground games where someone said, 'OK, this is the sea and there's the jungle' and that was all you needed for it to be true? A three-year-old who wants to be a dinosaur (and terrify her younger sibling) doesn't need a costume or app. She just imagines it, and it is so.

Imagination allows us to shape-shift and time-travel, fantasise and formulate.

In the context of daily life, another word for imagination is daydream. Whenever you are in one place and mentally drift off to another, you are using your imagination, and it's a wonderful tool for seeing and decoding connections in the world around you.

As Arthur Koestler put it: 'Man has an irrepressible tendency to read meaning into the buzzing confusion of sights and sounds impinging on his senses; and where no agreed meaning can be found, he will provide it out of his own imagination.'

I experienced this very powerfully, early in the genesis of Street Wisdom, when I was dwelling on how to sharpen my senses to better connect with my environment. For this experiment, I had written out a number of possible instructions, which I followed in a random order to see what the effect was. I had just passed along a street filled with stationary and padlocked bicycles and pulled out a piece of paper with the words 'follow the story' written on it. Suddenly the street was transformed. All of those stationary bikes were now two-wheeled narratives. Who were their owners, I started wondering? Where were they now? As I imagined further, the bicycles seemed less inanimate – more like tethered horses, each with its own rich unique 'story to here' and promise of 'destinations yet to come'. Three words had activated my imagination and the street changed. Suddenly, it was the perfect place for me to ponder my own forward journey. Synchronicity.

2. INTERPRETING

Imagination doesn't require belief. I can imagine a blue castle floating in the air above me without believing it's there. Interpreting suggests there's a meaning to be found 'out there' but that it needs to be understood, translated. 'The city is a stone book,' said Street Wisdom participant Donna Smithson. Yes, but we often find it's written in a language that needs an interpreter to make sense of it.

Just take a look at the second sign in the Arcade. It has a picture of a fish on it, plus a speech bubble and an infinity sign. What does that mean to you? To me, it's a reference to the Babel fish from Douglas Adams' *Hitchhiker's Guide to the Galaxy* – the creature that, inserted in your ear, allows you to understand any language you hear and turns you into the world's greatest interpreter. But it's a matter of interpretation.

Interpreting awakens the code-breaker in our minds. It makes us curious to find meaningful messages in the chatter and static of city life.

It's an invitation to explore further, go deeper than the surface that the city presents to us. Esperide Ananas Ametista, another of my long-time co-researchers, steps into view and puts it this way:

> 'Whether we realise it or not, we're always giving meaning to things. When you look up at night you see all these beautiful constellations – Pisces, Cygnus, Hercules. But these are just names our ancestor gave to shapes in the sky. Sometime, someone looked at a group of stars and said, "that looks like an arrow, let's call it Sagittarius." It goes into the culture and people start to think it's a thing rather than an interpretation.
>
> 'Does that have an influence on us? Sure, because there are mil-

lions of people reading their star charts every day who think it does and that in some way shades their perceptions. Do the energies coming from the cosmos exist? Yes. Are they called Aries, Orion, etc.? No. We gave these meaning because we experienced something happening when that particular constellation was in the sky.'

So how does this interpretation work on a walk through a street?

'Let me give a silly example. Let's imagine I have been dreaming of carnations all night. The next day, in the street I meet someone who is wearing a carnation like the one in my dream. I might do one of three things: first, not notice because I am still asleep and not living my life with much real awareness. Secondly, I could see the carnation and simply say how odd that it was in my dream. Thirdly, I get curious about the connection and start to explore to see what it might mean for me. That could lead me to a different way of thinking about a problem I have. It's a choice to connect the dream and the reality in my brain, mind and heart.

'I feel we are given different pieces of the puzzle. But it's a puzzle we can put together in many different ways. We can choose how we combine these elements to create different pictures of reality.'

My friend Marc Lewis, the educationalist and Dean of London's School of Communication Arts 2.0, uses Street Wisdom to help his students access the creative inspiration that's all around us. Like Esperide, he emphasises the active choice of the interpreter:

'Creativity is all about joining dots. But first you have to collect the dots to join.'

Good idea. Let's move on and join dot number three in our synchronicity safari.

3. NOTICING

Sometimes, when a participant is concerned they won't find the answer to their question on a Street Wisdom walk, I'll send them off with the reassuring words – *answers are everywhere.* Over time, that's become the strap-line for movement. We say it because it's true. Answers are indeed everywhere. The problem is, we just don't always notice.

As my photography teacher, Liz Handy, used to remind me, a great photographer could take a whole series of wonderful pictures without moving from the spot where they were standing. The less accomplished snapper (like me) would rush around the place seeking interesting angles and content, bending their knees and tilting the lens in clever ways, without realising a great shot was to be had right where they started.

Noticing is really important, and also a real challenge to our workaday consciousness filled with noise, mental chatter, trivia and to-dos. Often the answer we are looking for whispers to us and is drowned out in the sensory static.

I've had the pleasure of attending some inspiring courses given by the founders of Process Orientated Psychology, Arnold and Amy Mindell. At the risk of radically oversimplifying, they approach reality as a three-layered cake. On the surface there's Consensus Reality, a reality that is largely fictional, but which we all subscribe to as it's a way to get through the week without a nervous breakdown. Below that is what they call Dreamland, a domain where the Jungian collective unconscious exists. And below that is the profound and unknowable dimension of Essence. Arnie's view, and it's become mine, is that Dreamland speaks to us not only in sleep but also when we are awake. The conversation manifests in subtle signals, micro-movements of the body, fleeting presentiments. He calls these 'flirts' and has developed a complete practice built on the ideas of lucid dreaming and Zen Buddhism to help develop our awareness of them in daily life. You can read more in his book *Dreaming While Awake* but the essential lesson is that a deeper, more meaningful conversation with ourselves and our world is available, when we learn to notice.

As Robert Moss echoes in his enchanting book *Sidewalk Oracles*:

'Through synchronicity, powers of the deeper reality come poking through the walls of our consensual hallucinations to bring us awake.'

One of the ways this manifests on a Street Wisdom WalkShop is when a participant finds themselves at a junction or crossroads and feels, rather than decides, which way to turn. Keying into the intelligence of the body seems to guide us. The body's preference for one direction over another can be very slight, but if you reflect and feel your way, you will sense the direction in which opportunity lies.

Opportunity is the perfect word for this way-finding process. It is derived from two words: *ob*, meaning 'to', and *portus*, meaning port. So opportunities are directions that 'bear us towards harbour' – If we only notice.

Joseph Jaworski, who wrote an acclaimed book, *Synchronicity*, on the subject, has a different but equally gripping way of describing how synchronicity presents itself to us as 'a cubic centimetre of chance that pops out in front of our eyes from time to time'.

'The difference between an average man and a warrior is that the warrior is aware of this, and one of his tasks is to be alert, deliberately waiting, so that when his cubic centimetre pops out he has the necessary speed, the prowess, to pick it up.'

Again, the key to harnessing the power and magic of synchronicity is to stay alert and notice when it's offered to you.

And it looks as though the Arcade of Synchronicity is just about to offer us a new insight.

4. PLAYING

As I said, Arnie Mindell talks about flirts, but also flashes and beeps. I love these terms (and the Mindells' approach in general) because while the subject is arguably serious, the spirit is playful.

The Mindells practise the Zen concept of Shoshin or 'beginner's mind', an attitude of openness, avoiding preconceptions and an almost puppy-like eagerness for seeing the familiar with free eyes. Sessions with Arnie are frequently interrupted by the great man barking 'woof' in delight as he learns something new from a newcomer about a field he has created and worked in for decades. This kind of playfulness is, I believe, another way to tap into the creative resources that synchronicity is offering us on every street, every day, everywhere.

As the writer, actor, director, activist, part-time ventriloquist, inveterate trickster and irreplaceable creative, Ken Campbell, used to say (or, more accurately, snarl), 'this is all far too important to take seriously'. With typical provocation, Ken was reminding us that the more serious you become about the world, the realer it seems and the harder to change. Playfulness, by contrast, keeps our relationship with reality light and curious. Play with the environment, as we say at Street Wisdom, and it will play back.

A practised exponent of street play is Chris Sollett. You may remember him from that very first, rain swept Street Wisdom earlier in this book. He's now Street Wisdom's informal Head of R+D; that's Research and Development to you and I, but it's Rest and Downtime to Chris. Chris treats the street as his playfellow. And, as he explained to me, it returns the compliment.

'I was in Berlin and I thought I'd like to buy an instrument. But I wasn't sure exactly which one or where to find a music store. First thing the street gave me was a red and white felt tip pen.'

An artist by training and background, Chris likes it when the street gives him objects. And often makes sculptures with them afterwards.

'Anyway, the two-tone pen top set the pattern and led me to speak to some Croatian buskers; red and white are Croatia's national colours. They showed me where this music store was and I went in to buy an accordion. A red and white one. On the way back I met these gypsies again, had a cup of coffee with them and they gave me an accordion lesson. Also lots of compliments on my new instrument. Apparently it was a good one.'

Chris treats the objects he finds in a particularly playful way.

'I love it when the street gives me gifts. I am always picking up objects like screws and bolts, washers and pencils. If I find something like that, I will carry them around for days. I am not quite sure why, but it's like some sort of touchstone. I've start putting things back as well. But that's much more difficult for me. I leave them for where other people might find them.

'Now I think someone else is doing the same for me. Recently, in my village in Spain, I found three pairs of shoes in exactly the same place. Maybe it's a ritual or a game.'

Sometimes the playfulness turns into real game-playing.

> 'Another time, I was haggling for a chess set with a couple at the market and I noticed there was a pawn missing. They were suspicious that I had somehow pocketed the missing piece to drive down the price. I was miffed at the suggestion because the whole set was only two euro. And anyway I have about ten chess sets at home so didn't really need it. I stomped off, feeling a bit offended, and on my way home came across a pawn in the street; a symbolic pawn, at least. It was actually part of a white-painted bedhead, about 40 centimetres tall. I took it home and reflected on the message that might be here for me. Was I the pawn in this situation, being manipulated by the market traders? Or maybe it wasn't supposed to represent a pawn but instead a bishop or king? Maybe it was asking me if I wanted to play a more interesting role in life. I don't like to overthink these things or the meaning sort of dissipates. But the wooden piece is on the desk in my office and I reflect on it often…'

For most of us, buying a chess set would be just that – a purchase. For Chris, it was the beginning of a playful mini-exploration that led him to discover a perfect, discarded object, a sidewalk treasure, which in turn sparked a relevant reflection.

I think this is a perfect example of how playfulness opens us to synchronicity, bridging the world we see and the sensed world beyond.

5. SYNCHRONISING

How are you finding the pace of our wander so far? I ask because the pace we set for ourselves hugely affects our experience. When we speed along the street, we are less likely to uncover its treasures. By the same token, if we dawdle through life we do not catch the wave of excitement. We will be playing more with this idea later in our creative dawdle together when we come to the *Change of Pace* chapter. During it, we will meet a street musician and by matching our shared 'beat' we will co-create a moment of remarkable and unexpected street intimacy.

This is akin to the technique that's developed within the field of Neuro-Linguistic Programming called 'pacing', in which you create rapport with a stranger by matching the rate at which they breathe, or blink or move.

There's something about sharing tempo that seems instantly to create rapport between strangers. Witness the intense pleasure humans feel in the muscular coordination of activities like dancing, marching and carnivals. Synchronising with others is not only satisfying but crucial to our social coherence. In a world that's moving and changing as fast as ours, it's essential we find times and places to *keep together in time.*

This synchrony also appears to be a bridge to synchronicity. When you adjust your pulse to match that of the street (not your busy schedule), magic seems to happen.

This doesn't always mean slowing down, by the way. If you were dragging your feet through a Brazilian street party, you'd be less likely to have a vibrant experience than if you jumped into the flow and danced. But generally, given the frenetic pace of our lives, synchronisation usually means taking our pulse down a beat or two.

Experiencing the connection between synchronisation and synchronicity is easier than you may imagine. My daughter, Elsa, loves coffee but was riding her daily cappuccino a stretch on an art student's budget. Then she made a discovery. While queuing for her morning caffeine fix on the jam-packed, rush-hour platform at London's Waterloo Station, she started taking the time to ask the baristas how they were. She was genuinely curious, looked them in the eye and made it clear she was interested in their reply. What she didn't know was that each of the baristas have a 'gift coffee' they can give free to a special customer at their discretion. Elsa has become that special customer for the whole barista team and hasn't paid for a coffee all year.

Shopping of any sort is a great opportunity to synchronise. You could argue that it is its social function – an excuse to interact with other humans. Go to any street market or souk and you'll see the actual purchasing takes a fraction of the time that's spent in amiable chat and pleasantries, testing (tasting, prodding) the produce and/or haggling over the price. One of the reasons that High Streets around the world are becoming less vibrant is the fact we don't have – or more likely don't give ourselves – time to slow down and interact with the shopkeepers. It's all about speed, with optimised queuing and automated, self-scan, robotised checkouts designed to get us in and out of the shop as fast as possible.

One simple way to synchronise a little more with the experience is to follow Elsa's lead. Take a moment – a moment is all it takes – to connect with the person serving you. Be curious. Be appreciative. Be human. You never know what you'll get back in return. On one memorable Street Wisdom WalkShop, one of the participants was queuing at a sandwich seller's stall. He seemed a character and because it took some time to hand-make the sandwiches, she took the moment to ask his opinion about a question she was struggling with: how could she perform better at work? It turned out the sandwich seller had been, in a previous career, a concert promoter for, among others, Frank Sinatra. The perfect person to share some insights about performance and at the perfect time. Synchronicity.

Hopefully, it's all beginning to link up nicely. But don't worry if it's not. That's normal. And as I said at the start, the Arcade of Synchronicity would ask more and more of us as we walk on. Which brings us to...

6. RECOGNISING

One of the reasons synchronicity troubles our rationality is the lack of apparent causality. Synchronicity violates our sense of what is reasonably probable. We just can't see the connection.

But what if we did?

What if we were to think of everything as intimately connected to everything else? We wouldn't be the first. Hippocrates talked about the sympathy of all things, saying 'there is one common flow, one common breathing, all things are in sympathy'. The idea that everything is woven into everything else runs through the teaching of Taoism and Neoplatonism, as well as most of the world's indigenous wisdom traditions. But to accept that idea feels like challenging what science teaches us about the universe and our disconnected place within it.

'According to modern science we're just chemistry operating in a purposeless universe generated by random selection.' That's Jim Garrison. Remember him from the introduction? One-time head of the US-based Wisdom School of Graduate Studies and now President of Ubiquity University, Jim is keen to point out that scientific reductionism – the orthodoxy of our age – doesn't want us to see these connections:

> 'Scientific dogma has been taught as truth in our schools and anyone who goes against that scientific dogma is not allowed to publish in the mainstream journals and barely can get any jobs in the universities. The tyranny of the scientific establishment is more total than when the Pope a thousand years ago held the keys of Heaven and Earth in his hands. So what I am going to say is probably going to sound heretical – but that view of the universe is just not possible.'

He looks more like an imp than a heretic. Clearly he is having fun as he pulls out what looks like a very professional list of numbers.

'Let me give you a statistic. The probability of creating a single cell molecule completely randomly is $1:10^{8896}$. That's a 10 with more than 8,000 zeroes behind it. And yet they say our universe was created in a Big Bang by complete chance, 13.8 or so billion years ago. That's 13 with just 9 zeros. In that time pure chance is supposed to have produced all THIS?'

He gestures at the teeming, intricately variegated world around us. 'It cannot be random, I'm sorry.'

He doesn't look sorry – more like delighted. Because he knows if your starting point is to recognise that we're not here by chance, that we are all intimately interlinked ('Plotinus says the whole universe breathes together,' Jim adds), then reality opens up in a quite magical way.

Far from being an anomaly, synchronicity becomes a norm. After all, in a world where everything coincides with everything else, why would synchronicities not happen? Suddenly you are not labouring to make connections, you are just acknowledging the myriad connections that bind us to each other and the world, every moment of every day.

Notwithstanding Jim's critique of reductionist science, not all scientists are closed to the idea of interconnections. The Danish physicist Niels Bohr uncovered the phenomenon of non-locality. Entanglement, as it's more commonly known, proposed that once subatomic particles are in contact, they remain synchronised (influenced by each other) for ever and over any distance. At the time, very few supported Bohr's counter-intuitive breakthrough. Even a creative thinker like Einstein dismissed it as 'spukhafte Fernwirkungen' or 'spooky action at a distance'. But in the years since, quantum physicists have gone on to prove that this connectedness affects not only subatomic particles but entities all the way up the food chain, including ourselves.

When you take a look at an average street through the quantum lens, it looks less like a mundane passage from A to B and more like a scintillating, hyper-connected field of energetic opportunities. As Peter Merry puts it: 'An energetic system is anything that has a name and a boundary to it. That includes a street. It's a system with a material, relational and energetic architecture to it. It's an identity you can interact with and affect.'

Hold the idea that when you are walking through a street, you are entering an information field. And add the possibility that it not only affects us, but we affect it, because that's where we are heading next.

7. INTENDING

So here we are, at our seventh spot and what I think is the central question of synchronicity. When we experience an acausal coincidence (hopefully a pleasant and/or useful one), did it just happen to us, or did we make it happen?

I'll say now that I don't have a definitive answer. But my experience with Street Wisdom has convinced me it's a 50:50 deal, a duet, a synchronic *pas de deux* with us and the universe around us playing equal parts in manifesting synchronistic effects. I'd like to share some thoughts from some people who've thought long and hard about this to substantiate my own conviction.

Many of us will have heard of the 'observer effect' from quantum physics, which proposes that the observation of any phenomenon changes (however subtly) the phenomenon. Here's my friend and long-time synchronicity researcher

Esperide Ananas Ametista, to offer a down-to-earth angle on the effect of observation.

'When people come and say "something magical happened out there", it only happened because they were watching it. If the most wonderful thing in the world is happening behind my back and I don't see it, for me it is not happening. That's what they mean by observation changing the universe. Unless someone is watching, nothing is happening…'

So attention is key. But do we have agency? Can we affect the world outside ourselves 'merely' by paying attention?

'Quantum physics says energy always follows awareness. And this leads to manifestation. How? Because matter alone doesn't know what it wants to be. It continues being one way until we interact with it. The moment we interact – be it physically or by giving it attention – it changes. You could say matter is asleep, waiting for someone to play with it and say "hey, I would like you to be this or do that".'

I love the idea of matter needing a playmate – us – to give it direction. It's an idea that's deeply explored by consciousness researcher Lynne McTaggart in *The Intention Experiment*, where she shares the results of several ground-breaking experiments that 'suggest that the observer effect occurs not simply in the world of the quantum particles but also in the world of the everyday. Things no longer should be seen to exist in and of themselves but, like a quantum particle, only in relationship. Co-creation and influence may be a basic, inherent property of life.

'When someone holds a focused thought,' she suggests, 'they may be altering the very molecular structure of matter.' And the name of her book suggests that, for McTaggart, the intention of the thinker is key.

That's certainly been our experience at Street Wisdom. The intention of the participant has the greatest effect on the amount and coherence of the synchronicity they experience. That is the function of the question we encourage people to ask in the Quest phase. It gives direction, meaning and significance to the exercise. It's sending a message to the synchronic field that you are here for a reason and want to play.

It's hard to articulate so we often use the internet analogy where we liken the WalkShop's Tune-Up phase to booting up a search engine, and the Quest phase to typing in a search term so you can start to interrogate the vast database of wisdom that's all around us. If you didn't type a question into Google, it would just look back at you dumbly. The moment you indicate an intention – for instance, 'I want to buy double glazing' – the interface springs to life and sends you 41,600,000 possible answers. Trust me, I just tried.

The internet simile isn't a bad one, not least because it makes the idea of an invisible but vastly valuable dimension of information much more acceptable. After all, that's how most of us think of the Cloud.

You won't be surprised when I tell you that participants with fuzzy questions often get quite a lukewarm response from the environment. Meanwhile, those with a burning question and stronger intentions seem to conjure equal and opposite, synchronistic reactions from the word *go*.

That's something to bear in mind as and when you choose to harness the power of synchronicity and what it can bring, as well as this piece of cautionary advice from Esperide: 'Synchronicity increases probabilities but doesn't guarantee anything.'

It's worth mentioning here that our intention can affect but not control the world around us. A number of the more optimistic – or opportunistic – champions of intention have, in recent years, suggested it is a formula for *getting what you want*. They see – and sell – intention as a sort of quantum-physics-validated 'abracadabra' that enables you to snap your fingers and make your every wish come true. 'Our power at this stage of our species' development is one of *manifestation*, not creation. We're selectors of events, not creators of them.'

She motions us to keep passing along the Arcade with a final thought. 'If we could completely create the reality we want, manifest anything we desire, that would be terrible, given our level of evolution presently!' A fair point.

So those are the seven most common ways I have found to evoke synchronicity in our everyday lives.

- Imagining
- Interpreting
- Playing
- Noticing
- Synchronising
- Recognising
- Intending

But before we leave the Arcade of Synchronicity, I mentioned there might be one more aspect to discover. And, in many ways, it's the simplest of all.

CHOOSING

Synchronicity isn't a thing. It's a choice.

You're not going to enjoy the fruits of synchronicity unless and until you accept they exist. As Esperide puts it, using a food analogy entirely appropriate for an Italian:

> 'If you opt not to believe an avocado exists and that it's edible, you're unlikely to ever taste one.'

Another choice we choose to make – or not… For her the incidence of synchronicity in our lives is 'about how we choose we want to live'.

> 'Do we want to feel we are just objects, victims of circumstance? Or do we want to observe what's happening and choose to make sense of events? I feel we are given different pieces of the puzzle. But it's a puzzle we can put together in many different ways. We can choose how we combine these elements to create different pictures of reality.'

Even if you're not sure (and no one can be completely sure), imagine a world where synchronicity is real. It's a world where the everyday dimension of reality is just one of many, where your thoughts have effects 'out there' as well as your actions, where you can create the conditions for moments of grace more often, where what's outside and around you reflects what's within you, where magic isn't an illusion, but a facet of reality.

If you'd like to live in a world like that, then choose to accept synchronicity is possible and start experimenting.

People arrive at Street Wisdom with opinions, and leave, three hours later, with evidence. Proof, remember, comes from the word *provare*, to try. If you want to prove synchronicity to yourself, you just have to test it.

And I hope you find the approaches I shared above useful.

EXERCISE: THE HUMAN SHOW

What?

This is an exercise to help cultivate more synchronicity in your life.

Why?

We often miss synchronicities or refuse to accept them because, without proof, our minds are unwilling to accept that the right things are happening at the right time. It feels too staged – like we are the centre of the universe's attention – and that feels implausible, self-centred and a bit too much like the Hollywood movie *The Truman Show*, where an entire town was secretly choreographed around a central character. So, to elasticate our minds and allow more possibilities, let's explore how that might feel.

How?

Walk down any street imagining you were directing a film, starring you. All the buildings are scenery. All the people are professional actors and everything that happens is happening according to a pre-written script – everything. The traffic, the weather, the shops and their content. You can encourage this attitude by whispering to yourself, like your own personal, on-board film director, 'traffic lights turn to green – NOW,' just as they do so. Or, 'cue the lady with the pram,' when a passer-by like that appears. When anything unexpected occurs, smile inwardly and say to yourself, 'that's exactly what was supposed to happen at exactly that time.'

First of all, many people find this very pleasurable and entertaining. But just as importantly, it encourages our minds to see and accept a hidden choreography to daily life that we hadn't been aware of before. And that acceptance will encourage more synchronicity around you. Don't take my word for it. Try.

You can see a digital version of this exercise here streetwisdom.org/wanderful-exercises/

Wanderful

Wandering with Ken was never going to be straightforward. That's because we both do a lot of it. And he's generally one side of the world while I'm on another.

When we finally do coordinate, he is at home in LA and I am in Italy. So, this is going to be a virtual, online stroll. Being thousands of miles apart could be a problem were it not for Ken's famous ability to tell a story and transport you to wherever and whenever his curious mind leads us.

And yes, it's a little odd for us to be wandering when we are both sitting down, but our immobility turns out to be quite appropriate, because the importance of movement – or the lack of it – is going to be something of a theme today.

To kick off our journey (literally), Ken takes us back to 1954 and a park in Liverpool where he is knocking a football around with his dad.

'Until I was four, I was a strong kid, running all over the place. My dad was convinced I was going to be a professional footballer. He'd played as a semi-professional when he was young, so this wasn't an idle fantasy. I was number five in a family of seven kids and Dad used to say, "he's the one – he's got it." I felt it, too. As I watched football, I had all the instincts. My body understood how soccer worked.'

Ken was a quiet child. Knowing him today, it's hard to imagine him not having a lot to say for himself. 'I've definitely made up for it since!' he admits. 'I didn't say much. Partly because I had a lisp. I didn't even cry. Then one day, my mum came to pick me up from the speech therapist and I was screaming the place down. It was eerie. The doctor said it was flu, but this was in the middle of a polio epidemic and when I woke up next morning, I couldn't move. I've had kids myself and I can only imagine what a disaster this must have been for the family. Anyway, I was whisked off to intensive care and was in hospital for eight months. I was completely paralysed to start with. But polio is a bit like a fire in a fuse box, it just depends where it gets to. If it affects your respiratory muscles, you end up in an iron lung, and worse, you can die. I came out with calipers on both legs, crutches, a wheelchair, long blond hair and – a lisp. The poster child for cute. People spontaneously gave me money when they saw me.

'I was the only kid on our street to get polio, despite my attempts to cross-infect everyone. I thought "you're coming with me",' he chuckles. 'Anyway, that was the end of the footballer dream. My parents didn't have a plan B, but they were very clear. "There's no way you're ever going to make a living doing manual work so you've got to focus on your education."'

And focus Ken did. Not only on his own education but on ours too, becoming one of the world's leading thinkers and speakers on this most personal of subjects, a champion of creativity and an excoriating critic of educational close-mindedness.

'A lot of what I have been trying to do,' he explains, 'is ask if we can create education systems which are consistent with the principles of human flourishing. That's all about relationships, empathy, compassion. Seeing how things connect – not just disassociated and disconnected from each other. Schools are divided into subjects, the world isn't. Schools divide the day into forty minute sessions, life doesn't. Children in schools are divided by age groups. Outside, we don't tell kids not to mix with people of a different age. These are organisational, not human or epistemological principles.

'I was the one in the family under most pressure to get educated. And to be honest, initially I wasn't keen. This was the era of Beatlemania and we lived in Liverpool. My brother was in a rock band and they would rehearse in the next room to my bedroom as I was having to study irregular Latin verbs.

'I loved the precision of Latin,' he confesses now. 'I didn't love the precision of German, which I was also studying. The difference is that you have all weekend to work Latin out whereas in Germany people expect a response almost immediately.'

But the enchantment with education came early. 'When I was in elementary school, we lived in a small terraced house about two miles from the centre of Liverpool. Mum used to take me on the bus to where my calipers and shoes were made and just around the corner was this dark, crenellated, early Victorian building. I saw people swirling in and out in gowns and I was captivated. It was a school called Liverpool Collegiate. We didn't have Harry Potter back then, but to my young self that school was, essentially, Hogwarts.

'I was in special education at the time. If you had any kind of infirmity in those days, you went into Special Ed. There were only two types: schools for mentally handicapped and physically handicapped. They hadn't really got the hang of euphemisms back then. There were kids in my class with all sorts of difficulties – cerebral palsy, heart problems, partial sight... I think I said in one of my books, my class looked like the bar-room scene from Star Wars.'

Ken is no fan of educational metrics. 'I'm not against measurement per se. Thanks to measurement the house is standing up. We're talking over Skype because someone figured out the mathematics of the system. Numerical measurement is necessary but it's an insufficient conception of human intelligence.' However, it was the so-called eleven-plus exam [essentially an IQ test that's been used in the UK to assess eleven- to twelve-year-olds for entry into secondary education] that was his passport to a new world.

'I was coached through the eleven-plus and was the first person in my school to pass. When the acceptance letter from the Liverpool Education Committee plopped through our door, I discovered I'd been allocated to the Collegiate.

'I loved it. There was this big, oak-panelled assembly hall. And I was intrigued by the teachers. They would swarm up and down this central staircase like bats with their black gowns flowing behind them.'

But Ken's educational progress was about to experience another shocking jolt. 'My dad had an industrial accident. He broke his neck and was paralysed. We had to leave Liverpool for Widnes. That's about twelve miles outside the city – but a universe away. Liverpool was the city that gave rise to two great football teams, a generation of great comedians and the Beatles. Widnes was a small chemical town where the main sport was rugby league. We might as well have emigrated.

'So, at the age of twelve, I used to get a train every school day from Widnes to Liverpool Central and then get the bus up to school. Our classroom was on the fifth floor up these big, hard Victorian stone stairs. My calipers at the time were a bit primitive so I was getting all these pressure sores. It didn't bother me at all, but it bothered the teachers. They contacted my parents and said, "We think this is really too much for him." I was kicking and saying, "No no no I don't want to leave the school – I don't want to go."'

Ken was ultimately reallocated to the Wade Deacon Grammar School in Widnes, but his passion for education had been kindled. That said, the future professor had his doubts about classical academia even back then.

'Though I have written a lot about the limitations of the academic approach, I love academic rigour and I like the company of academics, but I just find it a limited view of intelligence and culture.

'I used to hang around in coffee bars and then pubs, talking about the Big Questions with friends, including my prematurely bald but precociously side-burned mate Alan. [Sidesy O'Brian we called him. Witty, I know.] I liked to debate with him but his default line to end any argument was "logically that doesn't make sense". One day I asked him why he was so invested in the idea of logic. His answer was "logic is the heart of intelligence". But is it? It seems to me that formal logic doesn't touch a lot of the things that matter most to us.

'This isn't to say I am against Reason. But part of what I have railed against in education is the preoccupation with a certain type of reasoning. The logical, linear process of building one idea on another and cross-validating them has been tremendously productive in our lives. It has its own beauty but it's an inadequate conception of how the mind works. There are other forms of apprehension and cognition that together constitute the full complement of human intelligence. There are all kinds of rationalities, within which different types of ideas may be entirely coherent. There's the rationality of a painting, for example. Logic can't tell you what blue means if you put it next to violet.

'Our preoccupation with one, limited form of reasoning has marginalised our capacities in other areas, which turn out to be at the heart of what it means to be a human being.

'A few years ago, the BBC did a programme where they took me back to my special needs school. Sarah Montague, the interviewer, challenged me on something I'd said in a TED talk – "dance is just as important as mathematics."

'She couldn't believe I was serious – after all, "How many children in school are going to go on to become dancers?" she asked me. I could have asked her, "How many kids doing maths are going to go on to become mathematicians?" But that's not really the point. Maths is invaluable in human culture in countless ways, as it were. But we are embodied creatures. Our intelligence isn't just between our ears; it's distributed throughout our bodies. If we are to educate people cognitively, spiritually, emotionally, physically, they have to move.

'In general education, kids should be moving and connecting. Student achievement across the board improves when they are

91

able to move. A lot of the problems we have in schools are to do with social awkwardness and fear, which can be hugely mitigated through physical activities and particularly dance. Of course, there's a lot about mathematics in dance and, as it turns out, various studies have shown that children who are encouraged to dance in school often do better at maths too.

'One of the problems in our Western systems of thought is that we're taught that thinking is essentially about making distinctions. Some Eastern philosophies see thinking as more often about making connections. What you and I do is as much about associative thinking as linear thinking. That's what the experience of walking around and being conscious teaches us. People are much more likely to think differently if they move differently. If you sit them in a circle and ask "what do you think?", they will go into their heads. That's why I love what you are doing with Street Wisdom. You get them out on the street and ask a different set of questions. They can't help being stimulated by the new experiences.'

Ken's journey has been a stellar one. But, as he points out, he had help. From a mum and dad ['they were fantastic']. And from an extended family ['funny, noisy, our house was basically mayhem']. But one or two people also showed up at exactly the right time. Without them, life might have been very different.

'I was sitting one day in the special needs class and this guy came in. He made his way around the class and ended up talking to me for a while. I didn't pay much attention but a few days later I was asked to see the head teacher and this fellow was there again. I learned later he was Charles Strafford, Her Majesty's Inspector of Schools for Special Needs. He had seen something in me – some potential – and told the school, "I think you should be pushing him harder." I was moved into a different class where the teacher – Mrs York – was a real tartar but brilliant. She coached me through the eleven-plus and

I was on my way...

'Charles later became a friend. He was an upper middle-class fig-ure, noted in the cultural scene of Liverpool. An ex-major, he'd served at D-Day. He was a real Francophile, too, bilingual with a house in France. And a bit of a gourmet. He made me my first ever properly tossed salad. Amazing. A very sophisticated, charming, urbane man. I'd never met anyone like him. It was as if he opened a portal into a whole new universe.

'I owe him! Him and Mrs York.

'People like them are so important. They are mentors in a way they may not even truly understand. Charles Handy is another. Inspirational. They're signposts to something, but they don't just show you the way but actually help you to make that step if you're willing to take it.'

We saunter on conversationally, but Ken is dwelling on those early years and the inspirational influence his father had on him.

'My dad was fundamentally a very optimistic guy. Very street-smart. Very funny. Not educated, but wise. Then came the industri-al accident. Imagine. Here's a working-class guy, very physical, who breaks his neck and suddenly he has no money, seven kids in a working-class house in Liverpool. He lived another eighteen years as a quadriplegic through sheer strength of mind and he spent those years as the life and soul of the family. You just wanted to be in this man's company.'

'Maybe it's because of him but I think I always had a positive view of things. I always thought that I would do something I found interest-ing and was important to me. I think it's who I was.' Ken didn't expect to be one of the world's most celebrated, in-demand [and, believe me, funny] speakers. But, as he explains: 'I have always had a thing about not walking away from things that frighten me. If there's some-thing that scares me, I tend to go towards it.

'The last thing I thought I'd be doing is standing up and speaking

93

to rooms full of people. But in 1963 our cousin Brenda was getting married. My brothers Keith and Ian and our cousin Billy decided to do a drag act, lip-synching pop songs speeded up to sound like Pinky and Perky. They needed someone to introduce them and I was suggested. I was thirteen. I overheard my parents saying, "Kenneth won't get up in front of a crowd like that." I thought, "You're bloody right." But I did. I didn't do too good a job, but I was up there – on my way.'

Our wander together ends where it began, with a four-year-old kicking a ball with his father. 'I knew I could have done the footballer thing. If I had, we'd probably be having this conversation in a sports bar. But life is a kind of conversation between circumstance and disposition, isn't it?

'There's that lovely line from George Kelly – in A Theory of Personality – Experience isn't what happens to us, it's what we make of what happens to us.'

6

Off the Straight and Narrow

'Logic will get you from a to b. Imagination will take you everywhere.'
Albert Einstein

**Ours is a complex, fast-changing world that requires us to
pivot, adapt and turn on a dime. Why, then, is straight-line
thinking still so deeply embedded in us and our culture and
how can we learn to wiggle more?**

As we're wandering together, I notice there's a tune playing
through a window somewhere. Do you hear it too? It's a
classic Sixties number. And it couldn't be more synchronistically appropriate for this chapter. Listen.

Oh yeah, I'm the type of guy that likes to roam around
   I'm never in one place, I roam from town to town ...
   Yeah I'm the wanderer
   Yeah, the wanderer
   I roam around, around, around

I think there's a good reason Dion's rock-and-roll hymn to wandering became a classic. A musical masterpiece it isn't, but it has a message that speaks to our soul. Somewhere ingrained in us is the lure of a carefree life, beyond routine and schedule, where we can traverse the world answering only to our own inner compass. In Dion's case, the goal is pretty girls, fast cars and the occasional bar fight. But we all have our own inner wish list that we'd pursue if we had the time.

I'm curious about what stops us wandering when the allure is so strong. Why don't more of us reject daily routine for the open road more often? I have less excuse than many. I invented Street Wisdom, for goodness' sake, so why do I often find myself feeling stuck in a hard-edged, time-boundaried world?

Is it just time that stops us?

I notice that people who do Street Wisdom often thank us for giving them permission to take some time for themselves, hit the pause button and wander. It's touching to hear, but why should we need permission?

Let's leave Dion a-warbling and spend a few pages together thinking about why we might get trapped – and indeed trap ourselves – into living a way that's straighter and more narrow than we'd wish. We'll look at some sources of our self-constraint and then see how we can release ourselves into something a little bit more wiggly.

A STRAIGHT LINE RUNS THROUGH OUR EDUCATION...

I remember my first school ruler. It was a twelve-inch strip of honey-coloured wood, neatly hatched with printed numbers and a shiny brass band at each end. More importantly, I remember how being given this mysterious object made me feel: grown up.

Farewell, childish scribbles. This was a first step into an adult world where chaos was to be ordered, the universe tidied.

From the get-go, our education encourages neatness. And the ruler is an unyielding edge to train our jumbled thoughts, words and numbers into obedient rows. In an educational world that reveres straightness, the ruler is a potent tool – a way to put a definitive number to an estimated length, an antidote to guesswork.

Even its name is powerful. *Ruler*. The one who is in charge, the setter of *rules,* a name that leaders of nations yearn to be called.

Looking back at my early schooling, many things now seem odd: seating kids alphabetically in rows, tinned tomatoes for lunch, mandatory rope-climbing, for a start. But nothing is odder than the way teachers insisted 'straight is good' while simultaneously teaching us – through science, geography, history, the arts – that the universe disagrees.

In Nature, nothing is straight. We've yet to find a perfectly cubed planet hurtling through the cosmos. Planetary orbits are elliptical. Space itself is sexily curved, pulled out of true by hidden gravitational forces so even when you feel you are on a direct route in space, relatively speaking you aren't.

Down here on Earth, all kids know that a toy thrown straight at your sibling actually has a curved ballistic trajectory. Trees are straight-ish, at best. Rivers meander – that's practically the only detail I remember from geography lessons. Water doesn't go straight, it flows round obstacles rather than through them, and nor does wind. Believe me, as an enthusiastic if unpolished amateur pilot, I know this to my cost. Follow a straight line you have ruled on a map without compensating for the push and pull of the wind and you'll end up miles off course. And given we are living on a ball-shaped planet, any apparently straight line drawn on its surface will, by definition, be a tiny bit curved.

As architect and futurist R. Buckminster 'Bucky' Fuller explained, 'Everything you've learned in school as "obvious" becomes less and less obvious as you begin to study the universe. For example, there are no solids in the universe. There's not even a suggestion of a solid. There are no absolute continuums. There are no surfaces. There are no straight lines.'

...THROUGH OUR SENSE OF MORALITY...

As we expand our vocabulary at school, we subliminally absorb the idea that straight is not only neat but morally good too. We know that because of the approving words associated with straightness: *Direct. Ordered. Unswerving. Level. Even. Aligned.* These are all words you'd be proud to have on your report card. Not so their unruly opposites: *Indirect. Disordered. Errant. Uneven. Eccentric.*

The connotations between *straight* and morally good continue out into adult life, where forthrightness (directly forwards) is praised and any sign of deviance (itself a word that implies non-straightness) can be labelled *twisted, screwy, bent.*

Going straight is what criminals do when they have renounced the evils of crime.

Regular, regulation, regulated, constant, consistent, plain, plain-speaking, even, straightforward, straight, unswerving, unbending, fair and square, ordered, aligned, downright, rectitude...

All related to straightness. The very word 'right' is, the dictionary tells us, is related to the Latin *rectus*, 'ruled', from an Indo-European root denoting movement in a straight line. By contrast, the Latin for wandering – *aberrare* – is the root of both *error* and *aberration.*

So, semantically and syntactically we are programmed to think that straight is good and wandering, quite literally, wrong.[1]

...THROUGH HOW WE CONSTRUCT OUR WORLD...

Whoever or whatever designed the universe seemed to have been content with wobbliness, waywardness and wandering. Then, humankind arrived, ruler in hand. Like an annoyingly over-optimistic DIY-er, we nudged Mother Nature aside and, whistling tunelessly, set to work on our planetary home improvements; as the Bible puts it making 'the crooked places straight and the rough places plain' (Isaiah 40:4).

In his famous picture of Newton, William Blake portrays this great scientific organiser and explainer of Nature holding a protractor. It's an ironic comment, of course. Newton is pictured in black and white, ignoring the swirling colours around him, blotting out the curly-wurliness of the universe in an effort to get Nature to conform to his linear rules.

Don't get me wrong, straight lines clearly have their uses. If you want to control the world, as the Romans did, you'd build roads die-straight rather than meandering to ensure your army marches[2] directly where you want them as quickly as possible.

---

1. One particularly bonkers association between right-angled and right-minded is the common phrase 'straight as a die'. Though taken to mean completely open and honest, it is actually derived from the smoothness of dice used in gambling. So, anything but honest. Puzzling. Literally.
2. The military have always been fans of marching in perfectly engineered lines, though I did hear from one ex-services friend that this is less about military

In construction, generally, the plumb line is helpful. Straight towers tend to stay up longer than slanting ones. Architecturally, the rectilinear can be aesthetically pleasing. Think of Palladio's crisp classical lines, the New York skyline or the unerring modernism of architects like Le Corbusier and Mies van der Rohe. But generally, straightness is more a matter of utility than beauty. As architect and environmental designer Giuseppe Boscherini puts it:

'Straight lines are not about enjoyment. They fulfil a functional purpose; getting from A to B. The term "vernacular" in Architecture applies to the kind of straight functional architecture that forms the backdrop of our humdrum life, the very fabric of our existence. It is not noticed or noticeable but then that's the point; it has a quiet, peaceful presence. As soon as there's a bend or curve we are surprised, we don't quite know where we are going, we can't see the end of the street – so there's immediately a sense of drama and expectation, as we follow the curve round. That will be true until the day "wiggle" becomes the norm and then the straight becomes the disruptive exception.'

Giuseppe's talk of disruption makes me imagine the frustration of contemporary urban planners[3] who create optimised, nicely engineered walking routes for the public, only to find humans deviating from the plan and creating their own referred ways through urban landscape. Just look at your own parks, piazzas and public places and you'll see the 'desire paths' snaking their way between popular destinations. Sometimes these are shortcuts, but often they also indicate where people prefer to walk

usefulness (it just presents a nice ordered target to the enemy) and more about checking which soldiers are sober and which are too drunk to walk in a straight line.

3. The whole notion of a plan – derived from the word for 'flat' – optimistically suggests the world can be neatly smoothed out into a manageable plane of just two dimensions. Good luck with that.

or avoid. Andrew Furman, a professor in interior design and architecture at the University of Toronto has spent many years studying these acts of civic resistance and suggests they are evidence of 'the endless human desire to have choice. The importance of not having someone prescribe your path'. Planners love to set 'rules as to how public and public-private spaces are used', he says. And desire paths are about 'not following the script'.

So, yes, a clean, straight line has its place, and beauty, but generally, looking around at our attempts to straighten out the Earth, you'd have to concede that our straight-lined attempts pale against the majestic lumpiness of the original. As the great Catalan architect Antoni Gaudí, lover of natural forms, put it: 'The straight line belongs to men, the curved one to God.'

...THROUGH HOW WE SEE THE WORLD...

Tap 'human echolocation' into YouTube and you'll find extraordinary humans like Daniel Kish who are blind but navigate the world through what they call 'Sonar Vision', essentially clicking with their tongue and 'reading' where they are by decoding how the sound waves reverberate back from surrounding objects. They are the (heroic) exceptions to the rule. By and large, most of us are fortunate to have eyesight and tend to use our vision as our primary means of navigating the world.

It was not ever thus. One can imagine that, in the past, our other sense systems were more fully engaged to help us hear, feel and sniff our way safely across the primal steppes – evading predators and tracking prey. Today, though, eyes tend to rule, and eyes love straight lines. Our eyes, fixed neatly on either side of our front-orientated face, tend to look straight ahead. We fix on a spot and command the body to go there in as direct a route as possible.

Think about blinkers, sometimes known as blinders, that are put on horses for racing or driving. With eyes placed squarely on either side of the skull, horses naturally have pronounced peripheral vision. Blinkers keep their focus straight ahead, on the winning line, avoiding any potential distractions. Recent studies show that children who spend a disproportionate amount of time staring straight ahead at a device screen start to lose peripheral vision. Their vision becomes literally narrower.

I hear this blinkered approach in the language of the modern boardroom, peppered as it is with *targets to hit, time horizons to reach, milestones to attain* and *'hills to take'*. Focus is prized and taken to mean single-mindedly narrowing one's field of view until a single end point blots out everything else, which is great if you're focusing on the right target. But what if you aren't? You'll expend a lot of energy getting to the wrong place. And what about all the creative alternatives you'll have missed along the way?

What if we were less sight directed and more soul directed? Hopefully, by the end of this book, that's a question you'll be able to answer for yourself.

...AND OUR VIEW OF SOCIETY.

Those who seek to lead and govern us prefer straight lines. Why else would they call themselves rulers? Or make rules for us? Regulation (from *regulus*... you guessed it) is the imposition of guidelines that we are all to follow in a uniform way – with rewards for compliance and punishment for deviation.

As Bruce Chatwin notes in *The Songlines*, his paean to the Aboriginal ritual of walkabout:

'Psychiatrists, politicians, tyrants are forever assuring us that the wandering life is an aberrant form of behaviour; a neurosis; a form of unfulfilled sexual longing; a sickness which, in the interests of civilisation, must be suppressed. Nazi propagandists claimed that gypsies and Jews – peoples with wandering in their genes – could find no place in a stable Reich. Yet, in the East, they still preserve the once universal concept: that wandering re-establishes the original harmony which once existed between man and the universe.'

But there's another reason society sees wandering as a threat. And there's a clue buried later in 'The Wanderer' when Dion sings:

Oh well, I roam from town to town
  I go through life without a care
  And I'm as happy as a clown
  I with my two fists of iron but I'm going nowhere

Wandering means rejecting the idea of a destination. But, if you're 'going nowhere', you're not being productive, argues our straight-line society. You have no prospects, and unproductive people are a burden. Wanderers don't fit the productive citizen mould.

And there's more. Not only is the wanderer 'going nowhere' but also 'from nowhere'. Stateless, rootless, and that's alarming. We're hardwired to want to know people's backgrounds. 'Where are you from?' is the age-old exchange between strangers. It's a basic way of assessing whether this is a potential friend or foe. Are you part of our tribe or a rival one? Hence our age-old reliance on second names – technically *toponymic* – which locate the bearer by their birthplace. Think of all those medieval-sounding names that link the bearer with their provenance: Catherine of Aragon, Eleanor of Aquitaine, John of Gaunt (so called not because he was undernourished but because he came from Ghent), Thomas Aquinas (born Tommaso d'Aquino – now Aquino near Naples), Francis of Assisi. Also there's those patronymic and matronymics that place a stranger in a recognisable family lineage. For example, Fernández (Spanish, 'son of Fernando'), Jónsdóttir (Icelandic, 'daughter of Jon'), bin Yousef (Arabic, 'son of Youseff'); even less obviously, Madison (Maude's son) or Marriott (child of Mary). Another way to identify who you are is to advertise what you or your family does – witness the abundance of names designed to advertise the family business (archer, baker, brewer, sawyer, slater, smith and so on).

It's an atavistic fear – this suspicion of the Other – but it's alive and kicking in today's nationalistic, political rhetoric too. The comment, 'if you believe you're a citizen of the world, you're a citizen of nowhere' sounds positively medieval in the way it collapses birthplace and identity, but was actually spoken by a British prime minister in 2016.

Rootlessness threatens social stability. Hence the suspicion that perennially greets the gypsy, the itinerant, the refugee. It explains why the term vagrant (synonymous with an untrustworthy ne'er-do-well) means literally *one who wanders.*

STRAIGHT LEADS TO NARROW

Education, religion, culture and society have all done a pretty good job of convincing us that life lived in a straight line is a proper life. But there's a catch. With straight comes narrow. If you let the linear become your habit, it becomes very hard to deviate when you need to, or when you want to.

Habits reduce options. That's what they are for. They enable us to complete repetitive tasks in a way that doesn't tax our minds and waste energy. We store our habits in our unconscious mind. It's like a huge memory bank with unlimited capacity. By the time we reach the age of twenty-one, the subconscious has stored one hundred times the content of the thirty-two volumes of the *Encyclopaedia Britannica*. It ensures you respond exactly the way you are programmed, with the help of its commander, the conscious mind. But in so doing, habits keep us stuck in our comfort zones and end up automating how we see the world. Life can become a little dull.

Think how commuting – tracing the same route to and from work – takes the edge off our energy. Being on autopilot may be efficient but it's hardly vibrant.

The good news is that, despite our best attempts to contain and constrain to restrict ourselves to the straight and narrow, the human instinct to wiggle is irrepressible. The wander will out.

BOULEVARDS AND BAUDELAIRES

When I am not out working with Street Wisdom, I spend a lot of time helping businesses think and act more creatively, and that, over recent years, has included several city planning projects around the world. They all have their own details and challenges but one overriding theme is livability – how to create places people want to live (for those people lucky enough to have a choice, that is). And at the centre of that challenge is the dynamic dance between control and freedom, where the impulse to constrain, direct and focus human activity – to straighten things up – meets the desire to encourage organic movement and individual freedom of choice.

Setting aside the megalopolises that are currently being built from scratch at the stroke of an administrator's pen in places like China, Africa and the Middle East, the world's great cities have tended to start small. Usually, where a chance geographical feature met a basic human need. The wide River Thames made Londinium the perfect spot for a Roman commercial centre to transport goods into the continent. The seven hills around Rome made the sheltered public area between it (the future Roman Forum) easy to defend, and Tokyo's large bay, known in ancient times as 'the inner sea', provided an abundant source of sea food.

Tim Stonor, of architects and urban planners Space Syntax, spends his life analysing how humans behave and designing cities around them. He describes city genesis[4] with a designer's elegance: 'Cities are where topography meets topology. Topography is what nature provides, and topology is what the human species creates upon it.'

No city better illustrates this, for me, than Paris.

In the third century BC, a Celtic tribe was looking for a good place to cross the River Seine, a site that could be easily defended from attack. Their name was the *Parisii* and the island they laid claim to was Île de la Cité, now home to the Pont Neuf and Notre Dame cathedral.

Over the following centuries, Paris gradually mushroomed out from that centre point. And mushroom isn't a bad metaphor, given the growth was organic, messy and, well, fun-

---

4. The Italian photographer Guido Guidi offers a delicious alternative account of how cities were first created and then evolved: 'The history of the city is like an egg. The ancient city was like a boiled egg, with clear edges bound by walls. Then the city became a fried egg, its edges spread out. Nowadays, it is a scrambled egg, with no form.' Guidi's beautiful images of the urban and suburban moments many of us miss are well worth a look . https://www.henricartier-bresson.org/en/expositions/guido-guidi-3/

gal. Forget the postcard-perfect capital we know today. Paris was noisy, traffic-crammed, foul-smelling, unhealthy, overcrowded, dark, dank and dangerous. 'Paris is an immense workshop of putrefaction, where misery, pestilence and sickness work in concert, where sunlight and air rarely penetrate,' wrote the French social reformer Victor Considérant in 1845. '[It] is a terrible place where plants shrivel and perish, and where, of seven small infants, four die during the course of the year.'

So, not exactly the destination beloved of tourists and teenagers we know today.

There had been several unsuccessful attempts to modernise the city, then along came Napoleon. A small man with big ideas and an engineer's mind, he proposed slicing through this heaving, unruly, urban bouillabaisse with a giant cross of dead-straight boulevards running north–south and east–west.

There was more than aesthetics behind Napoleon's concept of a *grande croisée*. Narrow winding streets are easy for dissident city dwellers to barricade, and barricaded they frequently were, in the numerous uprisings that convulsed nineteenth-century Paris. Broad, open and straight, boulevards are hard to block. They are also perfect for quick movement of troops to trouble spots and the easy manoeuvring of gun carriages. Apt, then, that the root of boulevard is military (from the German *Bollwerk*, meaning a defensive bulwark).

Napoleon had a good whack at straightening out the city. You can see what he had in mind when you look at the ramrod-straight north section of today's Rue de Rivoli. But he ran out of time. 'If only the heavens had given me twenty more years of rule and a little leisure…', he complained in exile, 'one would vainly search today for the old Paris; nothing would remain of it but vestiges.'

It's worth noting that a whole stream of modern Napoleons

have since sought to reshape their cities in order to impose authority on their citizens. Hitler, Mussolini, Stalin, Salazar, Franco, Ceauşescu all fancied themselves not only Masters, but master planners, and each of them, monomaniacally seeked to order the world to their will, opting for the purity of straight lines.

The task of modernising Paris was eventually taken up by Napoleon III and his uber-urban planner, Baron Georges-Eugène Haussmann. Haussmann was an aggressive moderniser who grabbed the dishevelled Paris by her absinthe-stained peignoir and whipped out his set square.

He completed the Rue de Rivoli extension in time for the Paris Exposition in 1855. Next came the two north–south boulevards of Strasbourg and Sébastopol, slicing unstoppably through the tenements and hidey-holes of old Paris. You can see the effect of his bulldozing in the numerous triangular-shaped islands of buildings, where Haussmann chose to chop diagonally through an existing city block rather than deviate around it. Cholera-riddled neighbourhoods were exposed to the air and light. Streets were widened, arcades installed, parks amplified and organised. Through the 1850s and 60s, Haussmann ploughed on, tearing down the old city and creating the Paris we know today.

The effect is beautiful. Gracious. Picturesque. Elegant. The citizenry is directed along routes the master planner has pre-meditated. Avenues lead to carefully choreographed vistas and points of interest. The stuff of postcards.

But that ordered spectacle is only half the story.

When you think of Paris, you also think painting, poetry, music, fashion, film. It's the city of Picasso and Diaghilev, Sartre and Georges Sand; the explosive, dark sensuality of the Moulin Rouge and Pigalle, the artistic ferment of Montmartre, heated philosophical debate in noisy, Gitanes-fogged cafes, sultry film noir. To find all this creative and cultural flora and fauna, you have to wander off the boulevards and penetrate the side streets, and when you do, you'll be following in the footsteps of another great Parisian invention – the *flâneur*.

At the same time that Haussmann was tidying up the town, a new figure was lurking in the shadows, observing wryly from the sidelines, winding their invisible way through the crowds, luxuriating in the aesthetic experience of urban life.

THE FLÂNEUR

The name derives from the old Norse *flana*, meaning to 'wander with no purpose', but that's not really correct. For the authors, writers, poets, musicians and philosophers who identified themselves as flâneurs, wandering *was* their purpose.

Baudelaire, poet and chief exponent of the flâneur movement, summed up the motivation of being 'a passionate spectator' with breathless excitement.

> 'It is an immense joy to set up house in the heart of the multitude, amid the ebb and flow of movement, in the midst of the fugitive and the infinite. To be away from home and yet to feel oneself everywhere at home; to see the world, to be at the centre of the world, and yet to remain hidden from the world-impartial natures which the tongue can but clumsily define.'

Street Wisdom participants often report they've experienced something similar: being simultaneously at the centre of things and invisible, seeing and yet not being seen, intensely public and private at the same time.

Where, previously, artists had typically headed out into the countryside to commune with Nature, Baudelaire and his fellow champions of flânerie (including Balzac and Flaubert) turned inwards, plunging into the roiling street scenes of Paris for their inspiration.

For Balzac, this wandering was a sensory feast, 'a visual gastronomy'. For the writer Victor Fournel, it was a kind of living photography, '*un daguerréotype mobile et passioné*'.

For Baudelaire, the clamour and busyness of the crowded, bustling city was not a distraction but an inspiration:

> 'Thus the lover of universal life enters into the crowd as though it were an immense reservoir of electrical energy. Or we might liken him to a mirror as vast as the crowd itself; or to a kaleidoscope gifted with consciousness, responding to each one of its movements and reproducing the multiplicity of life and the flickering grace of all the elements of life.'

The electrifying effect of the urban street would have become even more potent when, to mark the Exposition of 1878, Paris threw a switch and brilliant arc lamps lit up the night streets of the city for the first time. Suddenly, flânerie could be a nocturnal as well as a daytime activity.

The wanderer is suddenly transformed from outcast to undercover VIP, 'a prince who everywhere rejoices in his incognito', and wandering becomes a luxury, rather than a misfortune. 'The man who loves to lose himself in a crowd enjoys feverish delight that the egoist locked up in himself as in a box and the slothful man like a snail in his shell will be eternally deprived of.'

Dion would have approved!

A quick gender-sensitive note here. Though Baudelaire and his colleagues relentlessly refer to flâneurs as 'he', there's a rich tradition of women wandering. Possibly the best-known flâneuse is Virginia Woolf, who called her incessant city walking 'street haunting'. In an essay of that name, she talks about sailing out into a winter evening, surrounded by the 'champagne brightness of the air and the sociability of the streets' and how, when we leave the things that define us at home, we become 'part of that vast republican army of anonymous trampers'. Woolf, like countless flâneurs and flâneuses before and since, found that walking stimulated her creativity. She conceived her novel *To the Lighthouse* one afternoon, walking in London's Tavistock Square. And the very first line of her most famous character, Mrs Dalloway, is 'I love walking in London'. Spoken like a true flâneuse.

For me, these two intertwined stories of Paris, the twin tales of Boulevards and Baudelaires, say something really important about the living relationship between the straight and wiggly. Where a town planner sees urbanisation, the flâneur sees inspiration. Haussmann saw streets as a means of regulation; the flâneurs, of liberation. Traffic flow and creative flow can live side by side.

We need both. Too many straight lines and life is smothered. Too much doodling and nothing gets done. We need our direct routes. But, we also need to break their hypnotic power over us and step off the conveyor belt to have our own, self-directed journeys.

EXERCISE: THE FIFTEEN-MINUTE FLÂNEUR

What?

Experiencing the life of the flâneur – or at least getting a taste of it – is easier than you imagine.

Why?

This simple exercise forces us – gently – to override our habit of heading from start to finish in the most direct way possible. It's a way of initiating your neurology to slow down, your internal clock to stop counting down, and your body to wander – to fill up the journey from A to B with un-needed steps. The un-needed steps are the freeing ones; they represent the holiday you are giving yourself, away from the lockstep and the straight-ahead habits of modern life.

How?

Find a fifteen-minute gap in your day. If you really look, you'll find one. And if not, create one. The simplest way is to nudge two adjacent tasks away from each other in your agenda until fifteen minutes appears.

Find yourself a street – ideally a busy one, but that's not essential.

Think of where you are standing as point A. Then choose another (point B), which is a five minute relaxed walk away. Now set off for point B but give yourself fifteen minutes to get there. Yes, three times as much time as you need. The two-thirds of extra time you just gifted yourself is wander time, flâneur time. Spend it like a flâneur would. Imagine, as they did, you are taking a tortoise for a walk. Window shop, people watch, drink it all in. If there's a crowd, step into it and enjoy being invisible. Slow your pace. Head in the opposite direction from your destination, knowing you have plenty of time to get there. Observe. Be amused. Be curious. Take smartphone photos of things you haven't noticed before. (Phone on airplane mode, mind.) Maybe sketch. Make notes. Treat yourself to an absinthe – scratch that – cup of tea/coffee. With only half an eye, a lazy eye at that, on the clock, saunter, amble, loiter your way to your end point, enjoying the sensation of nearly being late for your own deadline.

You can see a digital version of this exercise here streetwisdom.org/wanderful-exercises/

'Just imagine that. You spend your life dangling up there in the sky!'

You can tell wandering with Suzy is going to be fun. Even before we begin, she's asking a window cleaner why he's wearing climbing gear and he points up to the tower block he's about to scale. To him, this is probably an everyday task, but after a minute with Suzy he is looking up into the heavens, seeing his work in a different light.

Imagining what other people's lives are like and sharing ideas to make them better is what Suzy is all about, and her enthusiasm is infectious.

It's a drab day, but Suzy is a blaze of colour: fuchsia coat and a scarf that's a shock of yellow around her shoulders. Who could be a more perfect walking companion than one whose second name is – Walker!

'Greaves was my married name. I got divorced ten years ago and thought about changing but Greaves was my byline and the name I'd written all my books under, so I left it. Then I turned fifty and I thought "I want my own name!" I didn't want to go back to my maiden name as I am not keen on that tradition of belonging to father or husband. I wanted a new one. I wanted to feel I belonged to myself. So I got all my friends together one evening and made an announcement. "Suzy Greaves is dead. And Suzy Skywalker is born!"'

Skywalker? 'Yes. That's my full name. But the "sky" is silent!'

As her name choice suggests, she's a *Star Wars* fan, though she's less drawn to the mythic Hero's Journey than that of the Heroine. 'It's time for the inner more than the outer quest. The Knights of the Round Table need to serve the Queen, not in a gender sense but energetically. We need to nurture things rather than be saying, "There's a dragon, let's kill it!"'

Her own journey to here [today she's the editor of *Psychologies*, one of the world's most successful and popular personal development magazines] has had its dramatic ups and downs.

'My parents died when I was a teenager. My father died a long horrible death of stomach cancer. My mum's death was much faster – just four weeks. I'd had this idyllic childhood by the sea. Dog, brother, mum and dad, and all of a sudden it was washed away.

'I had to figure things out quick. I was in free fall, but I knew there were "ledges of happiness" for me if I could find them. Self-development didn't exist then as it does now but that's the direction I headed. Tony Robbins. Therapy. Coaching. To be honest, I was completely sold. When your whole world has disappeared, when everything you knew to be right and strong has gone, then what do you do with the rest of your life? For me, the key to survival was growth...'

We've turned into a side road of small, independent shops and Suzy has stopped in her tracks. 'It is a sign!' she says, face wreathed in smiles. She's pointing to the window of an organic cafe where there is, quite literally, a sign, hand-painted with the words: We Grow.

Suzy is laughing. 'That's part of my theme for next year. Keep. Grow. Deliver.'

The cafe is tempting but it's too soon for a cup of tea. We decide to wander but commit to returning here at the end of our walk. Watching Suzy carefully, I notice she's not deciding a route but, at every corner and junction, letting the direction suggest itself.

But, as I am discovering, that's very Suzy.

'I love editing a magazine like ours, which is about all the different ways you can survive and flourish. There is no one way to do that. There are millions. My personal path was through therapy, self-development and coaching. I got really evangelical, but I had friends who'd say "I'd rather stick pokers in my eyes than go to a self-development workshop". Instead, they'd climb a mountain. Or go wild swimming. Or walk a dog.

'Some magazines are really preoccupied with conventional – and that usually means financial –success. You know the story: "once I was poor and now I am rich". I am more interested in people who are making success on their terms. That's about valuing yourself not based on how much money you earn but the quality of the life you lead. Personally, when I see someone really walking their talk, doing it, making it in the world; I turn round and look at them. That's got my interest.'

Growing up in a Yorkshire mining village, Suzy is used to being considered a bit of an eccentric. And her fascination with human development hasn't always been as acceptable as it is today.

'When I first started editing the magazine, everyone used to tell me *Psychologies* was their "guilty pleasure". Like development was something to hide. Things have moved on. For example, mental health is a huge conversation now and we make sure we always carry stories for people who are struggling and need to find their own "ledges" to rest on. In my experience, no matter how dark things get there is always a way to see and think about the world which is healthy. How do you manage to balance the light and the dark in your life?'

We're so engrossed in the conversation I don't notice that Suzy has turned the tables and is now interviewing me! Before I know it, I've talked about my own brushes with depression as a younger man – about how darkness is part of wholeness. I am sharing things I haven't spoken or talked about for a while. But Suzy is so easy to talk to and no subject is off limits.

'If you came to one of our features meetings it'd probably look like a therapy session. I'll be encouraging people to really say what they think and feel. Because the work is only ever going to be authentic if we have those conversations about what's really going on.'

Suzy's warmth for her team is palpable, and I sense it's mutual.

'When I first came to *Psychologies* I was a journalist but I had never edited a magazine. It's a real skill. Flat plans. Choosing cover stars. I had never done any of that before. They said we love your vision and we'll show you how to do it.

'I am the personality type that's always coming up with the next thing and the next and the next. The team will often say to me "great idea, but maybe not right now".'

I experienced Suzy's torrential creativity for myself at the very start of this walk. As we prepared to set off, I spent a few moments fumbling to get my recorder working. In that time Suzy suggested I turn this interview into a podcast, gave it a name, suggested a podcast platform, proposed some equipment I should probably invest in, mentally sketched a design and strategised a plan for creating and reaching an audience.

So no shortage of ideas there. Which is probably why Oscar is so important.

'Oscar is the office dog. He is fundamental to the team and to me. He's what keeps us all sane. We'll be crazy busy and the team will say to me, "You are just being too nuts. Will you please take Oscar for a walk? And come back when things are clear."'

So many people are looking to Suzy and her magazine to clarify how they negotiate their future. How does Suzy navigate hers?

'I have to be a bit careful here. I do feel like I am entering my Third Act but that can sound a bit too Bono [love him though I do]. I used to be all about goals and making them happen. Now I don't set goals. The Universe just laughs at me when I do. Instead I set an intention and stay open to receive the signals. That's what's so important about making time to wander. Life often whispers the invitation and if we get busy, we miss it. Then it really has to bang on the door, usually with some sort of crisis, as though it's saying "do I have your attention now?"

'I use my heart to help guide me. I'll ask the world "show me!" And then wait for what I call a Heart Leap. We all know those times where you are in the place you think you are supposed to be, surrounded by important folk and all the rest, but your heart is sinking. I am constantly looking for people, places, work, where my heart leaps. Where I sense we can help the world be a better, more loving, kinder place.'

Tea is calling. And we're nearly back at the cafe with that We Grow sign.

'All my friends make fun of me for seeing signs everywhere. But the truth is I constantly feel the environment is chatting with me. I am constantly looking for meaning in the world and seeing how things are patterned. *Star Wars* jokes aside, I do believe there's something like the Force – a kind of thing that knits us all together. OK, it might just be that what you focus on expands but when I step back and slow down and stop thinking about the "should", I do get the answers I am looking for. I'll find myself asking what comes next and suddenly there's a bing-bong on the doorbell and life delivers an answer. It's really magical. Scarily magical.'

Now we're both laughing. The instrument store we've just passed featured a drum kit with the word 'pearl' emblazoned on the front. And the bookshop we find ourselves standing in front of specialises in witchcraft.

Scary. And magical.

7

It Is A Sign!

'The city is a stone book.'
Donna Smithson, Street Wisdom partici-
pant

Humans have always looked to signs and symbols around them to better understand what's happening and foretell what may happen next. Where our ancestors divined meanings from the natural world, Street Wisdom shows we can learn to read answers in the rich symbology and stimuli of the modern cityscape.

Street Wisdom is designed to switch our attention outwards. The idea is to shift focus from our daydreams (and the waking nightmares our minds love to concoct for us) outwards to a present-tense reality, bursting with stimulus, ideas, answers and wisdom for us. But there's a very good reason we might want to shut that world out.

On my way to the cafe this morning (I love to write amid

noise and coffee), I was told to stop, go, turn right, mind the gap, exit, buy now, save, tap my credit card, keep out, pay attention, wait… wait… wait… walk, stand in line, tap my card, please give a tip and take my order to my table. No one actually said a word of this. It wasn't people talking to me, but signs.

In the city we're surrounded, encircled, bombarded with signs. Signs telling us what to do and, more often, what NOT to do. Where to go, what to buy, eat, drink, wear…

There's visual overload. But it's also deafening – inside as well as outside our heads. Recent studies[1] in cognitive science suggest that the vast majority of us have inner reading voices or IRVs. This means when we read words (including these), we hear those same words in our heads. Try for yourself next time you're in the street. Can you read a sign without hearing it? And if you do find yourself experiencing an inner voice, notice the tonality of that voice. More than likely it's urgent, insistent, bossy.

This background urban babble is distracting, but not new. Signs have been a feature of streets for almost as long as we've had streets.

SIGNS OF THE TIMES

Classically speaking, the first proper road was the Appian Way, which the Romans built in the third century BC to connect Rome with the strategically vital port of Brindisi, over 350 miles (560km) away, down on the heel of Italy. To let travellers know how near or far they were from Rome, the Via Appia was studded with a granite or marble column (colonna mil-

1. https://bit.ly/2YFmQBI

iaria) every mile. This idea of a milestone – a regular way marker – caught on, giving travellers a sense of the progress, speed and time to destination. Now when travelling, Roman parents were asked by their grumpy children 'are we there yet?', they had an answer to give.

Milestones don't just tell you your position but also the importance of your destination. The Via Appia calculated its distances from a Golden Milestone (Milliarium Aureum) bang in the middle of the Forum in Rome. One can imagine the travellers' excitement growing as the numbers counted down on their approach to what must have felt like the centre of the world. The fourth-century AD Byzantine Empire had a similar mile-marker monument or Milion in the centre of its capital, Constantinople. More recently, my own country calculated all distances from the ornamental cross outside London's Charing Cross station.

But how was the visitor to navigate a new town once they had arrived?

In our sylvan past, when we lived and died within the same walk-able area, street names were hardly necessary. We'd know 'the butcher is just past the third oak and then turn right past the Wise Woman but tiptoe because she has a bad-tempered wolf hound'. Increased travel meant more strangers showing up, and strangers need directions. So streets acquired names inspired by their position (Top Lane, High Street); topology (River Walk); inhabitants (Baker's Place) and local landmark (Church Close, Memorial Drive). Over time, the street names were confirmed by boards, tiles or plaques usually affixed to buildings at key intersections. The street sign was born.

Helpful to the wayfarer, signs became essential to the shop-keepers, producers, market traders, inn-keepers, craftspeople and a host of other marketers jostling to sell their merchandise to the passing trade of urban pedestrians.

The Romans and Greeks cottoned on early to the merits of proclaiming your wares with a written sign or, in the days before literacy was common, a symbol. The image of a goat was used to suggest dairy; a mule driving a mill, a bakery; a grape-encrusted Bacchus, a wine merchant. In medieval Europe, a stylised shoe marked out the cobbler; a saw or hammer denoted a carpenter; bellows meant a blacksmith. Less obviously, the symbol of a bush came to denote a tavern. Pharmacists and other healers drew attention to themselves with a mortar and pestle, a carboy (a large, narrow-necked medicinal bottle) or a snake-entwined Rod of Asclepius. Pawnbrokers displayed three coins, which evolved into the three globes we know today and barbers, from the medieval period on, marked their premises with a pole, wrapped in a helix of coloured ribbons. No one quite knows why, but it's probable this alludes to the fact that early barbers also performed basic surgery. The coloured ribbons symbolised blood (red for arterial, blue for venous) and the pole itself, a rod the unhappy patient would grip to dull the pain!

Some shopkeepers became really creative in their efforts to distinguish themselves from the competition. They would engage their customers' attention with witty signs that contained a coded visual puzzle or rebus. A trader called Cox might hang a sign showing two cocks, while a hare and a bottle signified you'd arrived at Mrs Harbottle's store.

Merchants added an additional dimension of textual noise to public streets by using spare walls and whitewashed spaces ('albums' in Latin) for advertising. In today's era of high-end artisanal shopping, you wouldn't be surprised to come across a poster for 'Jinan Liu's Fine Needle Shop: We buy high quality steel rods and make fine quality needles, to be ready for use at home in no time'. The surprise is this advert was printed nearly a thousand years ago in Song Dynasty China. The poster includes directions to the needle store and a reminder to look for the White Rabbit sign outside.

So, there's nothing new about advertising. But the scale has exploded in the modern era and with the advent of electric light and, more recently, neon signs, the Big Sell goes on in our towns and cities 24/7.

In the 1970s, a new word, signage, was coined to describe this 'use of signs and symbols to communicate a message to a specific group, usually for the purpose of marketing or a kind of advocacy'. Signage. Ugh. An ugly-sounding word for an intrusive, all-engulfing, manipulative concept.

Wading through a sea of competitive visual chatter, it's understandable that we tune out, turn up the volume in our earphones and stare straight ahead.

But wait. Let's hold it right there – in mid-step if necessary.

What if we were to think differently? Instead of screening out this visual and mental clamouring, what if we were to treat it as an invitation to have a conversation with our surroundings? Could we use these signs not for the benefit of the 'seller or teller', but for our own – as markers on our journey, waypoints for our internal satnav to follow? Could there be signs all around us, potent with meaning, pointing us towards the answers to our questions?

To find out, we are going to have to make a small, if profound, sidestep – from seeing the world literally to sensing it symbolically.

SYMBOLIC NAVIGATION

Today, the word symbol is most often used to mean the kind

of pictorial character or icon you'd find on your keyboard. But that's a very recent demotion for a very potent concept.

Derived from the Greek 'token', the word symbol means, at its simplest, something that stands for something else. A symbol may have a surface appearance but that's only the tip of the iceberg. Behind it, is a wealth of hidden meaning that's calling out to be interpreted and understood. As Jung put it, 'as a plant produces its flower – so the psyche creates its symbols'.

In a world that's become relentlessly physical, symbols call us to the metaphysical in a way that transcends what you can see, touch and taste.

For much of our history, symbols were how we humans sought to understand this perplexing world and our place within it.

Anthropologist Joseph Campbell, author of the great mythic compendium *The Hero with A Thousand Faces*, describes a symbol as 'an energy evoking and directing agent' and as 'a sign that points past itself'. The monomyth (i.e. common to all cultures) that he described as the Hero's Journey unfolds on a landscape peppered with symbols to assist protagonists through their adventure. To our ancestors, finding their way around a largely unknown and usually hostile world, symbolic language was the navigational language. A sudden flight of crows, a peal of thunder, the call of a wolf, an early snowfall, a snake lacing its way along a path – these are all symbolic events, containing deeper meaning, guidance and warning for the early wayfarer.

When we wanted to look deeper, asking existential (and logically unanswerable) questions about our origins and ultimate destination, again, we did this using symbols.

Where did we come from?

All creation myths are symbolic. The Ainu people of ancient Japan say the gods sent a water wagtail to find an island in the watery wastes of the universe and created our world with the beating of its wings. But they don't mean that to be taken literally. The Zuni people of New Mexico say we appeared on Earth after being released from a lightless prison deep beneath the soil. Again, that's a metaphor to help explain the ineffable. The innumerable tales of gods spitting, sneezing or ejaculating mankind into existence are, likewise, meant to be heard as proxies for a truth – workable representations of much deeper mysteries: symbols.

Where are we going?

Our forebears were also very keen to know about what the future held, and they developed a dazzling range of practices to decode symbolic clues about what was to come.

From the Greeks and Romans onward, we've sought to read portents of the future through the movements of birds (augury); in the intestines of sacrificed animals (haruspication); the configuration of randomly tossed coins (numismatomancy) or bones – specifically ox shoulder blades (scapulimancy); in the play of lightning against a night sky (astrapomancy); the movement of sand (abacomancy); the dripping of wax into water (ceromancy); as well as the behaviour of horses (hippomancy), rodents (myomancy) and/or ants (myrmomancy). My personal favourite is cromniomancy, the craft of decoding meaning inherent in the sprouting of an onion.

Collectively, all this 'mancying around' is known as divination. It's a term that sends our inner sceptic running for the hills, suggesting superstition, mystery and connecting with some hidden god or goddess. But pare away the smoke and mirrors and set aside the contentious term 'divine' and we discover there's something very sensible at work here.

How well do you know what you are thinking? Right now? The brain is estimated to think sixty to eighty thousand thoughts a day – that's thousands an hour – so in truth we aren't thinking any*thing*, but lots and lots and lots of *things* at once.

Divination, whether it's reading chicken guts, tea leaves or onions, is a way to help you read your own mind. Learning to read the signs around opens up a lively channel of communication with your own intelligence. Put another way, a conversation with the outside world helps you hear the discussion inside your head; looking out is looking in.

In that sense, Street Wisdom is a contemporary form of divination, an experience that takes you out of your head and into the street so you can penetrate the mystery of your own mind.

READING THE STONE BOOK

Donna Smithson is one of hundreds of Street Wisdom participants who've written accounts of their WalkShop experiences. Here's part of hers:

> 'I began to see past the crowded shoppers and my senses had been enlightened, I was tuning in to conversations, "hearing" dialogue and noticing the tones in that dialogue. I was attracted to the infrastructure and sheer scale of the architecture with the added notice of texture, colours and shapes of these buildings. As I considered my own personal question, I noticed how certain signs invited me to reflect on it and consider what I needed to do differently. I found the hour went by very quickly. I really valued having the space and freedom to be alone with my question and ponder answers to it through visual stimulation.'

She summed up her experience by describing the city streets as 'A Stone Book'. I love that description. The question is, how can we, somewhat estranged from our symbolist roots, learn to read the signs it is sending us?

The first thing to remember is that we spend a third of our lives in the world of symbols when asleep. For those dreaming hours, we occupy precisely the same symbolic world as our forebears: a world where everything (the people we speak to, the animals we meet, the images, sounds, colours, numbers, patterns...) stands for something else. Previous humans carried this symbolic awareness into waking life. We tend to switch it off when the alarm clock tells us it's time to get up, get real and get to work, but we don't have to, and, in many places around the world, they don't.

Travel somewhere like Bali, as I did last year, and you'll see offerings of flowers, seeds and fruit strategically placed on different compass points. The Balinese are just one of the many peoples still connected to the idea that different geographical bearings have their own symbolic power. Each direction in Bali – and there are eight (plus a central uniting one) – has its own sound, colour, symbol, weapon and deity associated with it. Your actions and intentions need to be attuned to these directions in order to succeed. Sign a business deal or start a relationship facing in an unpropitious direction and you're doomed to fail. It's an energy system every bit as advanced as a national power grid and the Balinese maintain it with their daily awareness.

The Balinese offerings, called *canang sari*, are, like much of Bali, beautiful, entrancing and highly symbolic. They suffuse the island with a sense that there is more going on than meets the eye. Everywhere is a portal to somewhere else. No wonder millions fly from their pragmatic cities to this tiny island every year in search of something other – to experience how a normal street or market can be both intensely practical but also suffused with invisible meaning.

It's easy to understand why we jet off to other locations around the world in search of the otherworldly – understandable, but unnecessary. Because, as an urban system like Street Wisdom is proving every day, when you look at the world through symbolist eyes, you can find the otherworldly right outside your front door.

That said, detecting and decoding the messages hidden around us takes some skill and attention. Which is why I suggest we spend the rest of the chapter looking at some techniques you can use in the streets to convert the vapid background chatter of signage into meaningful symbolic signs to help you better navigate life and work.

There are three principles I'd like to suggest you keep in mind as we embark on our sign-reading expedition.

Principle 1. The meaning's in your mind

Symbols won't always make sense at first look. You'll have to make sense of them.

Fortunately, we human beings are brilliant at seeing the meaning in things. For good reason. We have always been curious about what's going to happen next. We've had to be. Less swift, strong or ferocious than our many predators, nerdy *Homo sapiens* has bested a hostile ecosystem with a unique ability to connect unconnected information into a sequence of meaning.

Let me show you what I mean. Step into a theatre with me. In my day job as a creative advisor to companies, I often use theatres for workshops because in their pared-down, black-box simplicity they are designed to help us see some of the aspects of humanity that are masked from us in daily life. Take a seat and imagine I am on stage in front of you. You ask me to make a meaningless gesture. I choose something at random –

for instance, I lift up my left hand, move it left–right–left in a lazy arc and put it down again. Then repeat.

Meaningless, right? A tall bloke with a big nose waggling his hand in a mindless sequence.

But wait. Watch what happens if we dim the lights and add a spotlight, so I am now picked out of the background. Now add some music in the background. Try something sad. In my own head I am hearing Samuel Barber's *Adagio*, the film score from *Platoon*, but you choose your own. What do you see? Suddenly I'm waving goodbye, perhaps on a railway station, to a loved one or calling forlornly for help, stranded on a desert island. Or... or... or. Your mind immediately connects the action and music and creates a causal narrative to explain the connection. He is doing A because of B. And this makes me feel C. It doesn't matter the gesture, or the music. Abruptly change the music to thumping drum and bass. The guy on the stage is suddenly a dad, hopelessly over-aged and out of place in a nightclub, trying to refind lost youth – and failing. (Perhaps I am oversharing here...) The scene is suddenly comic. The action hasn't changed, your interpretation has. The theatre isn't happening on stage, but in your head.

Step back into the street and this meaning-making is happening all the time. I remember back in the 1980s, the *Guardian* newspaper made an award-winning ad called 'Points of View'. As you'll see, if you check it on YouTube, it shows three short clips of everyday street life. In the first, we see a young man with a crew-cut running away from a car that has pulled up on the kerb. Our minds tell us 'that's a skinhead (thug) running from the police'. Next we see him running towards a well-dressed businessman and grabbing his briefcase. 'Mugger!' our minds call out in alarm. In the third shot, the camera zooms out to show a pallet of bricks falling from a crane above their heads and the young man saving the older man from injury.

Our mind instantly rewrites the narrative as we realise we have been watching a Samaritan in action, not a thief. 'An event seen from one point of view gives one impression' intones the voice-over. 'Seen from a different point of view it gives quite a different impression. But it's only when you get the full picture you can fully understand what's going on.'

Quite.

Principle 2. A dog is not always just a dog

'It is what it is' is a circular phrase I am hearing everywhere at the moment, wherever humans are perplexed by the complexity of life and want to simplify things by shutting down the options. But when your brain tells you the street is the street is the street, you are going to need some willpower to stay open to the possibility that the street is far more, and to hold to the conviction that 'it's NOT what it is'.

Fortunately, even the most hard-headed realists can get there, and no story proves this better than this one from the hyper-pragmatic streets of downtown Manhattan.

Ed, to his friends, is a professional's professional. The epitome of a hard-headed, no-nonsense New Jersey boy who's made it big in the Big Apple. When I told Ed he and his legal colleagues were headed out into the bustle of a Manhattan rush hour to slow down, tune their senses and experience life through the non-conventional lens of Street Wisdom, his look said it all. Two hours later, that look had changed: still steely, but amused and somehow different. He'd left the office with zero commitment to the experiment. 'I'm not a hippy, I'm from Jersey.' Deciding to make proper use of his time, he whipped out his smartphone and started to call clients. Ten minutes in, he was brought back to the moment by a damp sensation in his shoe and spreading up his trousers. A dog had done what dogs do on Ed's leg. What happened next surprised us all. Ed took this as a sign. 'When a dog uses you as a toilet, he's telling you it's time to pay attention.' Ed holstered his phone, tuned in to the street and bumped almost immediately into a firefighter (Ed's brother is a firefighter) with whom he had a fascinating conversation.

But Ed's final point was clear. 'Sometimes a dog peeing on your leg is not a dog peeing on your leg. It's a sign telling you to wake up!'

Principle 3. Seek and you shall find

Having a question is the best way to encourage the street to offer answers. That's why Street Wisdom has at its heart a Quest phase.

Being curious throws a powerful switch in your mind. Suddenly you find meaning where you least expect it.

Let me share a recent example of my own. While writing this book, I took time off to run a Street Wisdom WalkShop for a group of students from the wonderful School of Communication Arts 2.0, where I am an occasional mentor. It was a big group in the maze-like location of Brixton Market, and my attention was, to be honest, more on logistics than learning. Once I'd finished leading them through the tune-up phase and sent them off on their Quest, I thought I'd embark on a mini-quest of my own.

My question was how to better handle an urgent issue that was keeping me up at night. Not global warming, Brexit or the fragile state of democracy (my wife worries about those). This was a really important issue.

I was outside a shuttered shop, leaning on a closed steel roller blind, looking blankly at a pedestrian crossing in front of me. Without moving, I asked the question. For a few moments nothing happened. Then suddenly the answer flashed in front of my eyes. Wait! And I mean, literally flashed. A pedestrian had pressed the traffic light button illuminating the 'wait' sign. A detail I might normally have walked past, but in my intentional, questing state, those four letters were sending me an unignorable message: be patient.

Mentally stepping back and viewing my current disturbance on a much longer timeline, I realised the issue might take a while to resolve and that pushing for a solution now would only increase stress.

But that wasn't all. Once I'd entered a zone of heightened meaning, the signs kept coming. With a jolt I felt the world move. More specifically, the roller blind behind me. As it turns out, the shop wasn't closed for the day but had been temporarily shuttered because someone had smashed the glass door. As I watched, a couple of workmen slowly and patiently, replaced the shattered pane with a new one. No muss, no fuss. Drama over, the shop recommenced trading. In case my mind hadn't registered the first message, the environment had sent a live, symbolic demonstration to confirm it. Wait!

Once you're on the lookout and you have given your mind an incentive to look deeper, you'll start seeing signs and symbols everywhere.

Let's try it. You ask a question you want a fresh answer to. And let's take a virtual, literary wander together.

You keep your eyes and ears open and I'll whisper some nudges in your ear.

Having spent years personally experimenting with Street

Wisdom techniques, leading events around the world and listening to what participants have discovered, I've got some ideas about the kind of signs we'll see and how you can best read them. I'll point these out as we go.

HEADLINES

A very common way the street seems to communicate meaning is through what I call a 'headline'; that is, a *line* of text, or single word that lands in your *head* with a whoosh of real impact. You'll see five main types on practically any street you walk down.

Street signs

Street signs are often fertile sources of meaning because, as we've seen, they have local history woven into them: a rich story. Also, they can hint at aspects of town life that can't be seen, but can be sensed. Take Fleet Road, near my own home in London. No, there isn't a navy for miles. The road is named for the hidden river that rises nearby and runs secretly beneath London. You wouldn't necessarily know this elemental force is running beneath your feet, but you might sense it.

I always feel it's a shame when town planners resort to a random name generator for new street names. Or simply an anonymous (1 2 3, A B C) grid system like New York City. I visited some friends who have a place on the Palm in Dubai recently. Some imagination has gone into this development – a palm-shaped artificial island that can be seen from space. Disappointing then to discover the creativity didn't extend to the choice of street name: Frond B.

Shop names

In my TEDx talk about Street Wisdom,[2] I talk about how

my daughter, Elsa, found herself in an unfamiliar part of town on an early Street Wisdom walk. Slightly overwhelmed by young teenage-hood, she used her WalkShop to ask: *How can I be more comfortable being less comfortable?* And the street had rewarded her with what she felt to be a powerfully meaningful answer. It was buried in the text of a public service poster warning of the dangers of unlicensed taxi cabs and read: *Always know your way home.* Absorbing this, she happened to look up at the shop sign and her jaw dropped. It read *E Pearl*. Her name. When you know she'd inadvertently strolled into Hatton Garden, London's jewellery district, the connection is more understandable. But for Elsa, the effect was an almost miraculous endorsement of her experience – and it's the experience we have that matters.

Advertisements

Advertisements are usually exhorting us to do something, so it's not surprising they speak directly to our psyche in engaging language when we're in Quest mode. I've lost count of the number of people who've been wondering whether to take a risky step in work or life and have returned from their Street Wisdom Quest having been 'told' by a hoarding or bus to 'Just Do It'.

Sometimes the ads really gang up and make their message unavoidably clear. One participant returned from her Street Wisdom Quest looking decidedly grumpy. She was at a major decision point in her life: changing countries (to South Africa), moving in with her boyfriend there and having a baby. 'These are things I have been planning to do, but I wanted to be sure, so I asked the street. Before I'd gone very far, I saw one after another, an advert for wedding dresses, baby food, cheap flights to South Africa and an ad (for patisserie) saying, 'go on, you

2. https://bit.ly/30Lhebn

know you want to!' So why the grumpy face? 'You had warned me signs might speak to me but I mean, come on. Give me a little wiggle room!'

Graffiti

Graffiti are a wonderfully rich class of signs, superimposed (literally scratched) on to the urban landscape by people who want to send a message to the passer-by. Here are a few road-side scribbles that were powerfully meaningful and timely for participants in recent Street Wisdom events:

- 'It's never too late to do something that you have always wanted to do'
- 'Tell him'
- 'Take risks'
- 'See love in people'
- 'Break glass to escape routine'
- 'Ahead Only'

Traffic signs

When you are looking for meaning, you'll be amazed how what was intended as an instruction to drivers, work as cautions, cues and coaching hints to pedestrians. Imagine you're thinking about a future challenge of your own and see what the following traffic signs might mean to you:

- 'No U Turn'
- 'Maintain Speed'
- 'Slow Down'
- 'Stop'

- 'Attention'
- 'Delays Possible'
- 'Caution: Speed bumps ahead'

Top of my own personal chart of public signs is one that jumped out at me from a street-side in Kyoto, Japan. Next to a symbol of a crossed-out hand it read: Please Do Not Anything. As wise as a Zen kōan, and just as perplexing.

WISDOGRAMS

When a visual message leaps out of the streetscape and burns itself on the retina, I call it a *wisdogram*. This has happened on every event I've led or taken part in.

One vivid example was reported by a participant in Copenhagen. It was a rainy, blowy day in the Danish capital, but Street Wisdom was well-attended. One of the participants, we'll call her Lotte, was at a crossroads in life, wrestling with a career change. Should she stay in a 'boring job' or take up a new career as a mountaineering guide? Her heart said 'head to the mountains' but there was a problem – a lingering health issue that could compromise her ability to do that high-stress, high-altitude job with safety. She returned from her walk looking subdued. It wasn't disappointment but shock. The signs had been equivocal about her career choices, neither for nor against. But then, thirty seconds before she arrived at the cafe where we'd all agreed to meet, she'd turned the corner in an alley and been confronted with a life-size picture of a shaman. Why so shocking? Because Lotte grew up in a rural part of Denmark where shamanism was practised and she'd been told since a young girl that she had a natural gift for it. This was not

137

something she had been willing to accept previously. But now, more mature, and seeking her calling, the street had thrown her a visual reminder, a third way forward in life that she hadn't been expecting and which, judging from her reaction, was one she was now going to consider.

Incidentally, many Street Wisdom participants like to use their smartphones to capture visual messages during the Walk-Shop and then post to Instagram. You can see some on our feed, @street.wisdom. I think of it as a digital blink. You might want to try this yourself out there on the street, but if you do, we'd advise you to switch the phone to airplane mode so you're not bothered by emails or text messages. For once, let's use the phone to help improve concentration, not distract us.

MEANING MONTAGE

Often, individual images will combine in a sequence (like a film montage) to tell a story or solve a problem.[3]

Jem, a successful but somewhat frustrated creative, came to Street Wisdom wanting to know: 'How could I make more money from what I love?'

Tuned up, he set off on his Quest with sketchbook in hand. He works in graphics so he's a strongly visual learner. On his Quest he saw and doodled: a beer glass outside a pub, a church spire, a green-cross pharmacist sign and the cover of a book about bees. Stimulated by the question, his mind organised these apparently disconnected images into a striking new idea. Outside work, Jem is a lover of beer, particularly

3. Before Jung came up with the word 'synchronicity' to describe how coincidences occur without any apparent causal explanation, his fellow Austrian, the biologist Paul Kammerer, coined the term 'seriality' to account for how and why life sometimes 'lines up' in this way.

craft beers. Prompted by the beer glass, he began wondering if his hobby might be the basis for a new business. But how to make it distinctive in a crowded market? The church spire reminded him of the flavoured beers made by monks down the ages. Prompted by the bees, what about a honey-flavoured beer? And how about focusing not on its power to inebriate, but instead – prompted by the pharmacy sign – health? Jem returned at the end of his walk, not only with a new business idea – healthy, honey-flavoured beer – but a black and yellow (bee-inspired) bottle design. Even a wordplay name for his new passion product: MedicinAle.

SIGNSATIONS

OK, it sounds a bit seventies' disco, but there's a class of communications the street sends me that I call 'signsations'. (I suppose Sense Signs would be equally good, but I quite like the glitter-ball, glam-rock associations of my preferred word). These are, as the name suggests, signs that speak directly to the senses, notably smell and sound.

Seductive smells (baked bread, coffee, spice, lavender, frying onions… OK, that's a personal quirk but mmm) can all act as 'walk this way' signs. That's why shopkeepers and cafe owners use them. Street Wisdom participants often report how an attractive perfume has led them to a discovery or a disagreeable odour has forced them to deviate from a planned route into something more interesting. It's like our metaphorical Stone Book has the occasional scratch-and-sniff page.

The olfactory bulb, where our brains analyse smell, is closely connected to our amygdala and hippocampus, neural regions that handle memory and emotion. Perhaps that's why smells so easily fire off associated memory. The aroma of tinned tomatoes instantly transports me back to my infant school. Newly laid tarmac puts me at my grandparents' house in Brighton in the summer of 1968. Can't help it. And pencil shavings? Geography exams. Keep your nose open for smells and the meanings your mind can read within them.

In his novel *Perfume*, Patrick Süskind describes his nasally gifted anti-hero Grenouille obsessively tracking 'a crumb, an atom of scent' through the foul-smelling 'thick gruel' of eighteenth-century Paris. A piece of overheard music can guide you in the same way.

SOUNDSCAPING

Our tumultuous city streets are awash with music – from stores, from cafes, from open windows, passing cars, buskers. It can be revealing to follow where that music leads you. I was walking in Paris with my daughter when we heard a distant snatch of jazz. Elsa's ears pricked up and she was off, following the twisting alleys into the heart of the Marais neighbourhood. There, a guitarist, bass and fiddle player were swinging through Hot Club of France hits as an eccentric older lady in gloves, hat and net veil did a shuffling tap dance. Romantic, delightful and quintessentially Parisian, it was something of a life-changing moment for Elsa, who fell in love with the city and is now planning to study there.

Music can do that.

LISTEN OUT FOR KLEDONS

A final form of aural signalling I alert you to is the overheard conversation. In order to make sense of things amid the background chatter, we tend to screen out irrelevant conversation around us. On Street Wisdom we encourage people to turn their attention outwards – and that includes their hearing. It's fascinating what you can hear – and overhear. Conversations can often have surprising relevance to the question you are asking. This is not a new phenomenon. The ancient Greeks seeking oracular wisdom would be instructed to whisper their question to a god's statue then close their ears, walk away and listen out for the divine answer in the chance words overheard from passing pedestrians. They called this form of eavesdropped oracle a *kledon* – an omen of presage contained in a word or sound – and it was one of their favourite forms of everyday divination.

UNBURIED TREASURE

The streets of our cities are not paved with gold, but they are crammed with treasure. When you are looking for answers, seeking insight, following the satnav of your soul, you will find your path littered with objects that carry valuable meaning. Even litter. Remember how in the film *American Beauty* a plastic bag caught in the updraught of an air vent seems to perform its own, beautiful air ballet? Well, on one walk which I was leading, a participant was triggered into a really profound reverie by watching how the light glinted on a shred of discarded plastic. Sounds trippy, I know, but it's remarkable how often Street Wisdom walkers return bringing quite simple objects that have guided them in their quest for answers.

Fashion mogul Sir Paul Smith tells a wonderful tale of a lucky charm he'd found discarded on the floor of Milan Airport. His flight had been delayed but unlike his fellow passengers, who all logged on to their emails, he went for a wander, found the charm, and thought it would make a perfect button for a new shirt he was designing. The shirt sold around 25,000 units.

Sometimes the connection is admittedly tenuous. Other times, it's supernaturally accurate. I witnessed an example of this first-hand when I was leading an event and my sister Jenny decided to take part. Jenny has six children. Five have left home and her youngest was growing up fast. The question Jenny wanted to ask the street – she won't mind me telling you – was about what she would do when Oryon finally left home. It's gratifying when family want to take part in an experience you've created, but also nerve-wracking. As Jenny and her fellow participants headed off into the rain on their Quest, I had a private word with the street, asking it not to let me down in front of my big sis. I needn't have worried.

As we sat in a warm cafe, drying off for the final phase of Street Wisdom, participants started sharing what had happened and what (if anything) they had learned.

When it was Jen's turn, she reached into her bag and placed what looked like a fat notebook on the table, slightly damp, with different colour inks running from the pages. Intriguing... She explained that she'd been walking slowly through the drizzle, paying attention to how the water was gushing out of the gutter pipes, when she noticed one seemed to be blocked. Curious, she reached in and pulled out this book. To be precise, a diary. Written by a woman, a mum, who – guess what – was thinking about what she was going to do when her kids left home.

What the diary was doing in a drainpipe and how it had found its way into the hands of the synchronistically perfect reader, none of us could explain. But we knew we were in the presence of a talisman.

SSHHH

What's remarkable to me, all these years into Street Wisdom, is not that people return from their WalkShops having seen, read and been guided by signs, but that these signs are so completely different, person to person. What is revelatory to one participant is trivial to another. A message I might walk straight past could be deeply significant to you.

And there's an important reason for this. It's something I don't normally mention to people until they have done quite a few Street Wisdom walks. So let's keep it between ourselves.

You are not walking through the street – you are walking through 'you'.

Remember those subjective stories of the world that occupy our mind? They mean we decode every experience from our own personal, subjective viewpoint. What we encounter externally in the street, the signs we read, the images and objects we find significant are decided by our internal filters. What I see out there shows me what I am thinking in here.

The signs I encounter in the street help me navigate my internal landscape. It's me talking to me.

And that's the beautiful thing I've discovered about this street practice. It helps you see what's otherwise invisible in yourself, to reveal the thoughts you didn't know you had, to read a story that you are unaware you are living.

Yes, the street is a stone book and its pages are open to all. But the story you read there is wonderfully, intimately, revealingly your own.

EXERCISE: A SIGN, A SOUND AND A SYMBOL

What?

An exercise to help you better 'read the street'.

Why?

The world around us speaks to us in many ways, including signs, sounds and symbols. But our everyday sensitivity might not pick up the message, or decode its meaning, without a little practice.

How?

Think of a question you want an answer to. Find a street to practise in. Take a pad and pencil (or smartphone) with you.

Wander for five minutes and note down at least one written sign (e.g. street sign, shop sign, advertisement), one sound you hear (overheard conversation, piece of music, street sound) and one symbol (picture, shape, diagram) that COULD be the answer to the question. If you feel you are struggling to make the connection, that's fine. You probably are. But you are working muscles of perception that probably haven't been used this way for a while – if ever.

You can see a digital version of this exercise here: streetwisdom.org/wanderful-exercises/

'So, I bet you don't know what day it is...'

Like a lot of Gib's provocative questions, this is delivered with energy, humour and a gentle Scottish burr.

He's got me. But then I look up and see a huge, digital Scottish flag revolving slowing around a skyscraper on the horizon. Ah, St Andrew's Day, the day when Scotland celebrates its patron saint.

So the perfect day to meet Gib. Who is a Scot. Born and raised on the wildly and windily beautiful Isle of Bute. So a Scot's Scot.

But he's right. I didn't know. And it certainly wasn't something I'd consciously planned. But that's the kind of synchronicity you get used to if you spend time with Gib, a man who seems to live from one happy accident to another.

Synchronicity is practically the first thing out of his mouth as we stroll through the commuter crowd. He's explaining how he's buying a farm near his birthplace to turn into a business retreat. The farm miraculously came on to the market precisely when an unexpected property sale of his own meant Gib had exactly the right money to meet the asking price.

'I don't want to be some lazy capitalist squeezing money out of a buy-to-let. I want to create a place where capital could be put to much better use in the community where I grew up. I want to create a new place where business people can meet with artists, with musicians, with Nature. There will be no hierarchy – first names only. I want to get these dormant intrapreneurs, these change-makers working within companies to bring about innovation, to co-work and co-live for a day, a week, a month and then transplant them back into big business and see what happens.

'Everyone is talking about business accelerators. I want this to be a business decelerator.' And as he says this, he checks his step. He's been walking faster than me – a habit, he says, that he's developed in his years doing business in a town where 'everyone goes three times

146

faster than they need to'. As soon as he notices, he slows down to a congenial amble, and it sparks an idea.

'How long can you hold your breath for?'

I have no idea why Gib is asking but I agree to test myself right there on the pavement. While I'm holding my breath, going gently blue, a friend I cycle with at the weekends pedals past. I wave, mumbling a greeting behind clamped lips. Never seen him in town before. Just another synchronicity.

After what feels to me like heroic minutes without air [*it's actually thirty-five seconds, David*], Gib explains what's behind the impromptu lung test.

'You know where I was this time last week? Free-diving with dolphins in the Red Sea just off the coast of Egypt near the border with Sudan. I kid you not. Fascinating stuff. I was being taught by a world champion. She's the sort of person who can go down 104 metres on a single breath with no tank.'

Gib points out what that depth looks like by comparing it to a nearby tower block. Just imagining it is enough to make me hyperventilate.

'What's super interesting is getting to the point where the body can override the mind. First time I went down, I stayed under hardly any time before I started to panic. My brain is screaming "you're going to die, Gib!" In truth, while carbon dioxide does build up, you actually have plenty of oxygen. The problem is your mind. So they teach you techniques to allow your body to break through the mental fear. Meditation, relaxation, confidence building. A day later – and not because I am anything special – I was able to follow the guide rope gently down to about 10 metres, let go and sit on the sea bed with dolphins playing around me. Amazing. I don't know how long it was, and I don't care. It was a very, very powerful lesson about how my body can override my learned behaviours. We have this ability to survive even if our minds are telling us we're going to perish.

'It's a metaphor for so much in our life really. The head is telling you "follow the herd, make money, when you have enough money you can do whatever you want to do". We all chase this gold at the end of the rainbow hoping when we get there we're going to be happy...'

We've stopped walking and are chatting on the spot as a steady stream of passers-by flows round us, and as I listen, I get the sense that this is a lesson Gib has learned the hard way.

Five years ago on the same street, Gib would have probably looked like one of those busy people dashing by on their way to an important meeting. You'd have guessed he was a typical, high-powered businessman and you'd have been partly right. High-powered, yes. Typical, no.

Gib is an intrapreneur – a self-confessed 'corporate insurgent'. It's the subtitle of the book he's just published, which tells the story of his roller-coaster road to here. Essentially, he's a 'change agent' who has spent a lot of his professional life working to change business from within. Where does the revolutionary spirit come from? Maybe it's the islander in him, or the fact that a severe bout of alopecia, marked the twelve-year-old Gib out as physically different from the other kids.

'My career was anything but planned. I followed the herd into Engineering, then Mars via an MBA, all with making money as my North Star.' A life as a top-flight consultant engaged him for several years but soon Gib's intrapreneurial, countercultural attitude started him asking questions about purpose-driven business and how doing good well could be allied with doing good. He set up, led and ran a hugely successful new business line at Accenture called Accenture Development Partnerships or ADP, as it became known. Gib describes this as a 'not-for-loss' business that sought to bring the company's business and technology expertise to parts of the world with the greatest need but traditionally least access. To use

148

a line from *Star Trek*, to boldly go where the traditional pro-bono consultancy models had not gone before. It was a pretty unique business model.

'People thought I was nuts. Who will give up half of their salary voluntarily, they said? Why would Accenture forgo profit? What charity is going to pay for services it's used to getting for free? But it worked. Show me another company with over 50,000 employees queuing up to take a salary reduction and work in some of the poorest countries in the world.'

He bucked the trend, challenged received wisdom and succeeded – very significantly. But at a cost. Gib's drive drove him into what appeared to be a breakdown.

'Perhaps the people who told me I was crazy felt vindicated when I landed myself in hospital. Even I questioned my own sanity. But on reflection, is it so crazy to suggest business has a broader role than making money for shareholders? [1]

'I realise now you cannot look at the mental health of the individual in isolation from the health of the organisational system in which they are working. If we had companies that were a bit more purpose driven, actually contributing to making the world better rather than frying the planet, we might be happier, more engaged, less burned-out people.'

The breakdown turned out to be a breakthrough. Convinced some of the fundamentals of current business are actually insane, Gib exited the corporate world.

'To be honest, I stumbled out... it was not an elegant departure, and really scary at times. When I wrote *The Intrapreneur* I made myself very vulnerable. I remember the day I had to decide whether to kick off the book's crowdfunding campaign or not. I was in a hotel room in Chicago, looking at the laptop screen, wondering what I should do. Lawyers had been warning me that everyone was going to sue

4. Clearly the New York Times doesn't think so: https://nyti.ms/3fwQ6kO

149

me for what they assumed would be a whistle-blowing-style book. I heard my mother's voice worrying "you're going to lose everything". I'll be honest, I was scared.'

But then synchronicity struck.

'Out of the blue, I saw an email pop into my Inbox. It was an encouraging message from a friend of mine called Grant, who had literally stared death in the face – and laughed. It made me take a look at myself dithering. And I hit "send". I dedicated the book to him.

'He would have laughed at what happened next. I walk downstairs to the opening of the conference and the lady I find myself paired with asks me a random question from the suggested list of ice-breakers. "When was the last time you conquered your fears?" I looked her in the eye and was able to say, "About six and a half minutes ago!" It was a cathartic moment.'

We're winding our way past some university buildings with no particular place to go. Gib is now a free agent, advising, teaching and mentoring those who want to reshape the corporate world. So, what's the grand plan?

'No idea, and I am fine with that. I am letting things emerge. Take the farm. Everything in my training said "don't splash out on a pile of bricks without a proper plan – work out the commercials". But I overrode my conditioning. It sounds a bit "woo woo" but I am finding the right doors open and help seems to come when I need it.'

We're sauntering past a taxi stand where some London cabbies are parked up and taking tea.

'I tell students, don't be the black-cabbie leader in an Uber world. Don't be a Blockbuster behemoth when Netflix is round the corner. Unfortunately, the leaders of tomorrow – the people now taking their MBAs – are learning yesterday's Knowledge. They need to write their own script.'

We've found ourselves in a quiet park – a slice of peace in the noisy city – where the neatly criss-crossing paths intersect at a gushing fountain at the centre. Gib looks tempted to dive in and try some dolphin breathing but his attention is drawn to a gaggle of toddlers in school uniform. Hand in hand, they are being shepherded along by their vigilant teachers. It's a touching sight in a way, but Gib points out they are walking in an ordered, straight line.

'Children are the future, but the conditioning starts early. See, these kids are being taught to follow the rules at school. That will take them to university, and then they'll follow the rules in business. Wouldn't it be great if one of those kids broke away and headed off in their own direction? Everyone would be shouting "That's the wrong the way! If you go off there, you'll get lost."

'But we really need that kid. The one who is willing to walk away from the crowd and get into trouble...'

His voice tails off. I think we both realise who he has just described. And he's right. We do.

8

A Change of Pace

**Fast has become the default speed in our high-velocity
lives, but it's much easier to connect with the wisdom the
street offers when you are not hurtling past it. That said,
slowness alone isn't the answer, consciously choosing your
tempo is.**

Are you a fast reader, consuming whole books in a sitting?
Or maybe you like to savour them in small bites? Perhaps you
want to zip through this chapter or kick back and saunter
through? Whatever pace best suits you is fine with me, because
that's what this chapter is about. Living life at the speed we
want, not at the speed others want us to go.

David Pearl

A CULTURE OF SPEED

It's a truism to say the world is accelerating. Even discounting the distorting effect of our nostalgia for simpler times, the pace of our lives feels like it's faster by the month. Labour-saving devices that promised to help us do more work in less time have just created more work. Spaces where we could potentially catch our breath between tasks are quickly filled with more tasks. There's more to consume too. More to divert, amuse, entertain and 'edutain' us. FOMO (fear of missing out) has become the characteristic of our age – pressuring us to hurry from one experience to another at growing velocity.

Just look at the street. And the way we head where we're going like manic White Rabbits – late, late, for our very important dates.

Some time ago I was working with the operators of Stockholm's Arlanda Airport to see how the travellers' experience could be enhanced. My favourite observation spot was the end of a moving walkway where sliding glass doors smoothly hissed open to admit newcomers to the Arrivals halls. Not the most exciting spectator sport, you'd think, but... wham! Every so often a passenger walks full tilt into the doors with a crunch and a torrent of swearing. 'American or Brit' I chuckle, like a triumphant birdwatcher. These doors were timed to open for the laid-back Swedes, not harassed, urgently driven Anglo-Saxons.

The last time national walking speed was studied,[1] Singaporeans were the global pace setters, scurrying about at an average 3.9 mph, New Yorkers came in eighth, registering at walking pace of 3.4 mph, narrowly leading London at 3.36 mph. At the other end of the scale were the chilled citizens of

1. From a 2007 international study by professor Richard Wiseman of the University of Hertfordshire.

Blantyre in Malawi, who clocked in at 1.98 mph. That means they took a full 31.60 seconds to cover the 60 feet of pavement the researchers were clocking – some serious dallying.

Ominously, all cities in the study had increased their walking pace by at least 10 per cent (and in the Middle East/Asia, far more) in the previous ten years. So whatever beat your town or city naturally moves to, you can be sure it's increasing.

There appears to be a link between velocity and productivity, with the fastest growing economies scurrying about quicker than more slower growing ones. But while economists might approve of all this speed, your doctor probably wouldn't. Faster-paced cities tend to have higher rates of premature and stress-related deaths. It appears that hurrying will get us where we want to go faster – but also where we *don't* want to go faster.

Death, the Ultimate Destination, isn't something we necessarily want to stop and think about on a rainy Wednesday morning between dropping off the kids at school and racing to work, and that's one of the reasons we hurry about the place – so we don't have to think about the potentially troubling stuff. We've become dedicated to what the Dalai Lama calls 'active laziness' and 'housekeeping in a dream'. We're busy looking busy, tending to the illusion so we don't have to pay attention to reality, focusing on our feet rather than scanning the horizon.

As we reach what feels like terminal velocity, we are looking for ways to hit the brakes and rediscover a slower, more human pace.

One area where the tortoise is definitely hipper than the hare is food. The Slow Food movement, with its distinctive snail logo, emerged in Italy in 1986 as a reaction to the bland uniformity of fast food, specifically the McDonald's intention to open their first Italian 'restaurant' by the Spanish Steps in

Rome[2]. The movement has since grown across the world and the call to savour life at a less hectic pace has spread far beyond food into fields like fashion, medicine, science, travel, education, town-planning, gardening and investment. Slow Living is an emerging lifestyle choice, sparking a whole range of subsidiary explorations that include slow parenting and, perhaps unsurprisingly, slow sex. In all cases, the emphasis is not purely on speed but on the quality that's available when you approach these endeavours with a less frantic, fast-is-best attitude.

Someone who knows more about the topic than most is my friend, the writer, Carl Honoré. He's the author of *In Praise of Slow*, a book the *Financial Times* described as being 'to the slow movement what *Das Kapital* is to communism'. And he's ambling beside us now.

Carl was a late convert to slow.

> 'I used to be a speedaholic, stuck on fast forward.' His moment of 'sharp epiphany' came while he was reading bedtime stories to his son. 'My version of Snow White was so fast it only had three dwarves! One day I was online, about to purchase a book of 60-Second Bed Time Stories, and I realised this was ugly and unedifying – not what I wanted to be as a person or a father. It made me hit the brakes and consider what I was running from.'

Carl is a journalist by background, and there's a word that speaks volumes about our accelerating age. Derived from the French word for day (*jour*), journalism reminds us that news used to be a business of *daily* editions and deadlines when people could wait a whole twenty-four hours to find out what had happened in the world. Today, we want to know what is happening as it happens – preferably before. The news cycle has

2. https://nyti.ms/3d6ZfyT

accelerated to the point where publication is continuous, and the idea of a daily paper seems a quaint throwback.

Carl started to look for ways out of what he calls 'the forest of fast'.

'It became clear to me that speed is an instrument of denial, it doesn't leave you time or space to confront the bigger questions. Instead you're asking, "Where are my keys? I am late for my eleven o'clock meeting." Velocity masks pathology. Psychiatrists tell me the final stage before burnout is one final spurt of acceleration.'

The essence of *In Praise of Slow* is, as he puts it, 'savouring the hours and minutes rather than just counting them. Doing everything as well as possible, instead of as fast as possible. It's about quality over quantity in everything from work to food to parenting.'

There's a real allure in this invitation to step into the slow lane and enjoy the scenery for once. But when we try it, we often encounter a force field of resistance that keeps us stuck in fast track. 'Slowing down', Carl warns us, 'often requires a small rebellion.'

There's push-back from our culture, which doesn't rate 'slow' as worthy of respect. When were we congratulated for making slow progress as a child? When does a boss thank us for taking lots of time to arrive at a solution? In our full-steam-ahead culture, slow is a byword for stupid, dozy, dim or dumb. As we've seen in other chapters, we're encouraged to get where we're going as quickly (and in as straight a line) as possible, not by 'dilly-dallying along the way'.

Also, to slow down we have to break some social norms. We see this every time we run a WalkShop. There's a tacit rule on the streets that decrees we should move at the same pace as everyone else. Perhaps this is why the convention-flaunting flâneurs of the late nineteenth century were known to take to the Paris streets leading tortoises on a leash. Try slowing to a snail's pace in a Manhattan rush hour and you'll quickly discover what it feels like to violate the unwritten rule of Keep Up!

In some places, taking your own sweet time (rather than striding onwards) has actually been made illegal. Strictly speaking, loitering means simply 'the act of walking slowly and with no apparent purpose'. Law enforcement sees it rather differently as 'to stand or wait around *with the apparent intention of committing an offence*'. In other words, people with no apparent justification can be assumed to be plotting something nefarious. The UK's Vagrancy[3] Act (passed in 1824) lists a bewildering range of people who can be arrested for walking slowly without obvious purpose. They include fortune tellers, exhibitionists, promoters and players of Games of Chance, obscenity mongers... and others besides. Effectively, no one was safe from possible detention. Small wonder we learned to keep our heads down and our pace up in public.

As we saw in *Tuning In,* Street Wisdom encourages participants to hit the pause button and slow... right... down. The effect can be startling. Everyone has their own experience of this exercise. Here are just three.

> 'When we got to the Slow. Right. Down. bit, we found ourselves doing it together, walking up a set of stairs like a Spaceman and Spacewoman heading into a shuttle. It was, actually, mind-blowing. Ten minutes felt like about half an hour, honestly. It was incredible. It felt like stepping out of time. The German word for walking – 'spazieren' – shares the same etymological root as the English word 'space'. And in those ten minutes of Slowing.

---

3. Vagrant and vagabond are both pejorative terms linguistically derived from the verb 'to wander'.

Right. Down. it really felt like we had made more space for ourselves, for our lives, for each other.'
Philip

'How do you fall back in love with the place you once adored?
By slowing down and paying attention, it turns out, and taking
the time to look up, seeking quietude in a church or the clinical
emptiness of a new building, and connecting with people.'
Claudia

'I suddenly found myself totally excited about a weird fruit I've
never seen before, read books you could only read with a loupe,
played on a kebab slot machine, appreciated how all the fresh fish
were lined up in different colours, imagined the stories of all the
different people around me and enjoyed some old trees waving
in the middle of the street. I did not only feel totally captured in
time and place but also found myself with no thoughts at all and
still absorbing everything in a completely new way. THAT made
me feel alive.'
Christine

EMBRACING SLOW

As Carl puts it, slowing down in this way 'makes you more
alert and alive to what's going on around. You become the person in the crowd who does notice what's going on, the smells
in the street, the shifting of the light, the way conversations
ripple across a few tables along the pavement. Initially, it can
feel a bit like a sensory overload. That's a reason why some
people can baulk at doing it. But the payoff in my mind is so
handsome I think it's definitely worth persisting with and practising.'

Choosing to slow down doesn't just alter the way you relate
to the world around you. It changes how that world relates to
you. I had an indelible experience of this two-way effect when

I was practising my own slow-walking on a street in London's Shoreditch. Concentrating on slowing down my every movement, I noticed a pavement artist with a didgeridoo over to my right. Tie-dyed and dreadlocked, he was doing something of a 'crazy' act, trying to attract attention and contributions. I am a musician and artist, so technically this stranger and I are in the same tribe. But in 'normal' life, I know I would have sped right by him, partly indifferent and partly a little wary of his antics. When you really slow down, you start to notice people carry an energetic field round them, a sphere of influence that extends out from the body into the surrounding area. As I entered the hippy's energetic territory, he fell quiet. He watched as I approached and then, at precisely the same time, we both opened our arms. Without a word we hugged – very slowly – and then – equally slowly – parted ways. To a passer-by, this chance street embrace may have looked insignificant, but to me it felt seismic. By simply slowing down I had found a simple – and beautiful – way to connect without judgement or words.

Slowing down also helps us tune into what's going on *inside* ourselves – the inner space we also block out with incessant speedy activity. I am reminded of the pivotal scene in *Pretty Woman* where Richard Gere, playing the sharkish businessman Edward, breaks his relentless deal-making routine and, to the amazement of his chauffeur, heads to the park, takes off his shoes and stands barefoot on the grass. The short scene is pivotal and wordless. It's not about how Edward relates to the world, but to himself. Stopping the clock and slowing right down is making him think and feel differently. OK, falling in love with Julia Roberts (Vivian) may also have something to do with this, but the final shot of Edward contemplating his bare feet is telling us there's more to life than the sharp-elbowed merry-go-round of daily business life.

When a meditation teacher asks you to *notice your breathing*, they are guiding your attention to a steady beat within you. Holding on to this gentle rise and falls helps us be less distracted by the frenetic chatter of our minds.

The same is true when you find time to slow right down – even for a few minutes – during a busy day. It's another of the little acts of rebellion, telling the world: *Whatever pace you are going at, this is the one I choose.*

It can take some courage too. As my colleague Louise Cox Chester, CEO of Mindfulness at Work, puts it:

'By slowing down to the body's natural tempo and becoming aware of what it feels like to be a living, breathing, moving being in this always-now moment, the mind can come home to what is real and true, powerfully opening to the wisdom within and around us. However, inherent in this lies another challenge. Being present in our own lives often demands courage. Life can be tough, very tough at times. It's sometimes easier to allow ourselves to be distracted, letting our devices or other people hijack our attention and effectively checking out of our own lives. So if we are going to slow down and be mindful, we would advocate accompanying this courageous act with "kindfulness", bringing to ourselves the warmth and care that a friend might show us in that moment.'

MASTERING THE PACE OF LIFE

Clearly, slowing down is powerful. But there's more.

As pleasant and occasionally trippy as slowing right down might be, we're not recommending you spend your day that way. It wouldn't be practical, but more importantly it's not necessary.

Too often the idea of being present and mindful is confused

with slow and quiet. Most of us live in cities, not temples. And fully living in our urban setting has to be about engaging with what's going on around us, not screening it out. The real aim here is to be mindful at any speed, meditative amid the noise and rush, not just the wind chimes and whale song. Mastering the pace of your life starts with being aware of the pace of the world around you. Then deciding if it's a pace that you want to synchronise with. If it is, great. If not, set your own beat, and follow that.

You don't have to be stuck in the fast lane. Or the slow one. You can choose. And as you are choosing the tempo that's right for you, here are a few creative side streets you might want to explore.

1. Which slow?

Like much in our lives, the idea of pace has been oversimplified. Like the hot and cold taps of speed, just two terms – *fast* and *slow* – are used to describe an infinite range of different paces, from glacial to hypersonic. Just as Inuit can distinguish the single word 'snow' into multiple distinct forms each with its own name, there is a group of people who are skilled at discriminating minute deviations in pace. If you want to know snow, ask an Inuit. If you want to know *slow*, ask musicians.

Musicians' lives are ruled by time, or *tempo*, as they call it. The speed of a piece of music radically changes how it sounds to the listener. A funeral march sounds funereal because it is played at a stately pace. Speed it up to disco pace and it would completely change in character.

Technically, there is an infinite number of tempi to choose from, but the music world has settled on around twenty steps graduating from *grave*, meaning very slow, through *andante* (walking pace) and *allegro* (fast), on to *vivacissimo* (very lively) and finally *prestissimo* (hang on to your hat). It was practical to use Italian for these terms because that was the language most European composers had in common in the seventeenth and eighteenth centuries when this system was being worked out. But I think Italian is also a benefit because it makes all these different speeds sound equally wonderful.

And that's really the point here. Each of these tempi are distinct and characterful in their own way. None is better than the other. They are a palette for the musician to choose from. That's something to remember as we walk down the street. We can choose from a whole range of paces and all of them are good.

Carl agrees. 'Fast is not bad. And slow is not good. The slow movement is not about doing everything at a snail's pace, that would be absurd. There are times to be fast and times to be slow. The key is choosing the right tempo for the right situation, what musicians call the "*tempo giusto*": doing things at the right speed.'

And in case this is sounding New Agey, he points out that the *Economist*, bedside reading for the titans of capitalism, agrees, concluding an extensive report on time management in business with the simple statement that 'mastering the clock of business means knowing when to be fast and when to be slow'.

And when you do choose to decelerate, remember there are many flavours of slow to choose from, including:

- Lento (slowly)
- Larghetto (rather slowly)
- Adagio (stately – literally 'at ease')
- Adagietto (faster than adagio but slower than andante)

- Andante (walking pace, literally 'going')
- Andantino (a bit faster than andante or a bit slower, up to you)

You might even want to try a bit of slow marching (*marcia moderato*) or dancing (*tempo di valse*).

In short, get to know *slow* like the Inuit know *snow*.

2. Fast and slow

We have much more than *fast* and *slow* to choose from, but do we have to choose at all? What the last few years of Street Wisdom have taught me is that you can be fast and slow at the same time.

Again, this is an insight musicians are familiar with. Some instruments get a lot of notes (flutes, harps, piccolos) and others (including the bass clarinet, glockenspiel and triangle) don't. For many years I played double bass in orchestras and the bass is one of those 'fewer notes' instruments. If you look at the music parts of the average symphony, the violin part will be black with fast-moving notes while the bass part is liable to be mostly empty with patches of evenly spaced plonks and the occasional boom. A piece of music seems to proceed at several different speeds at once – and the sense of pace depends where you are sitting in the orchestra or band.

We see the same effect in our lives. Our physical experience is multi-speed. As you sit there, notice how your thoughts are fizzing around your head at the speed (literally) of light. Distinctly more leisurely is your heart rate, and steadier still is the pace at which your lungs fill and empty. Plodding along far in the rear is the rate at which your nails, hair and – slower yet – bones are growing.

So, the pace of life depends on which part of life you are paying attention to. If you're in the middle of a Kuala Lumpur rush hour concentrating on hailing that last available cab, the pace feels frantic. If you're in the same rush hour crowd focusing on your breathing, or the way the morning sunlight is playing with the jacaranda trees, the pace can feel serene.

Most of the people we meet through Street Wisdom feel they can't practically slow down their life but want to find a less frantic pace within it. Our recommendation to them is to *find the slow beat in the fast day.* That is to say, *act* fast while you *feel* slow.

Why would you want to?

Well, as Carl points out, this quality, a combination of speed and slowness, is a quality of high performers. 'The great players in all sport all share one hallmark, that they never seem rushed – they always have enough time. I think perhaps because they have an internal clock that's moving differently, an inner calmness that allows them to negotiate the fast moments with a stillness on the inside.'

Also, the ability to be unrushed amid the rush is a valued aim of mindfulness. As Arianna Huffington puts it: 'Life is a dance between making it happen and letting it happen.'

The luxury of the slow beat.

Another way to choose a slow pulse while in a fast life is to give yourself a project that isn't intended to produce instant results. Hobbies work like this, so does picking up a new skill. It's a way of reminding your neurology to be patient; to ween it off the serotonin squirts of instant gratification.

Smart companies do this too, counteracting the addiction to quick wins and fast turnarounds by thinking much longer term, about succession and legacy. One friend of mine, Marc

Mertens, founder of the agency A Hundred Years (100yea.rs), only works with clients willing to think a century ahead.

'Having a long time frame like this, one that exceeds our own lives, shifts our perspective,' he explains. 'It connects us with our purpose – crystallising why we are here and what we want to be remembered for. It challenges us to ask, what does the world need to thrive a hundred years from now, and what am I doing today to create that future?'

3. Take time to take time

I'll never forget the slightly frazzled young woman who joined one of our earlier WalkShops in Amsterdam. She had been on a professional career path, stepped out to have a baby and – had twins. Remembering how overwhelming one child was for my wife and I, the idea of starting parenthood with two is truly humbling. Trying to adjust to this lifestyle tsunami, this lady had come to Street Wisdom to ask, 'Where can I find time for me?' No surprise there. The surprise came at the end when she returned to share her experience. As often happens, the question she had originally asked had morphed during the experience. What this heroic new mum had found herself asking was, 'What does it mean to be a mother?' Not something she'd had a moment to consider since the birth. As she slowed down and refound the time to absorb the sights and sounds of a lovely Amsterdam spring morning, the answer came to her. 'The role of a mother,' she told the group with a smile, 'is to create great memories for her children.'

I love that observation. It's inspired me in my own parenting. Create great memories for your children. You can't do that if you're hurtling through life. The slower you go, the more memories you'll make. For all the smartphone pictures we take and Instagram images we compile, those memories tend to remain external. Platforms like Facebook can package them and play them back to you, but if you haven't really experienced them, embodied them, the memories won't stick.

That's one of the reasons I started drawing. Sketching requires you to take the time to really look. And when you really look, you really see. A tree isn't a uniform green. Two sides of a stranger's face are far from symmetrical. A discarded wrapper can be fascinating. A long airline flight is suddenly a chance to explore perspective, colour and tone. (Carl and I discovered we both like to sketch on aeroplanes. If we happen to be on the same flight as you, please excuse the quality but understand the intent.)

Slow right down on any street, any time, anywhere and you'll find experiences waiting to be turned into memories. There's always a story somewhere, lying dormant, waiting to be experienced. If it's not obvious, just take time. If you want your life to be full of stories to tell, *dwell*. In Carl's parting words:

'You gain a richness of experience when you slow down. You live life more fully, live moments that would otherwise pass you by in a blur. At slower pace they stick. It gives more meaning to life, more texture.' More memories.

EXERCISE: WALK, DON'T RUN

What?

A simple exercise to appreciate the power of slow.

Why?

There are myriad opportunities, even during the most hectic day, to pause and savour a slow moment. But we often miss them. This exercise invites you to make the most of wander time when it presents itself.

How?

For this exercise you will need a city street (the more traffic the better) and a traffic light/pedestrian crossing with any kind of walk/don't walk indicator. In many countries the sign is a green or red walking man.*

Press the button to indicate you want to cross. Wait, patiently, until the traffic stops and then saunter across the road as slowly as possible. Enjoy every step. Imagine you're crossing a field or a forest glade, not a busy thoroughfare filled with fuming cars and drivers. The idea is to use every single second before the green man turns back to red and the signals tell you the road belongs to the cars once more.

Be sure you cross safely, but smoothly and with panache, like a swan. While the green man shines, this is your time. Enjoy it to the full.

*Why always a man? Hats off to the organisers of London Pride, who managed to convince the authorities to install walk/don't walk signals featuring male, female and transgender symbols. They were meant to stay for a few weeks but are still there three years later.

You can see a digital version of this exercise here: streetwisdom.org/wanderful-exercises/

It's officially spring in Sydney but up here on the thirty-fifth floor the weather looks threatening. Despite that, when I suggest to John that we get out of the office and go for a walk, he grabs an umbrella and we're in the elevator sliding back down to street level. The office is pretty nice, by the way. All curved walls, open plan and espresso machines. But even so, John loves to get out and walk – by himself, with colleagues, and, increasingly, with clients.

As we amble past Moreton Bay fig trees towards Sydney Harbour, I ask him about the value of getting out of the office, even a lovely office, for a walk. John is setting a nice easy pace. He's a low-key, laid-back individual. You wouldn't necessarily know it if you passed him in the street, but he's something of a force in business, leading the Australasian activities of one of the world's leading management consultancies. So I guess it's not surprising his answer is organised into three well-thought-out points.

'First, it's very hard to go for a walk and take a hundred-page PowerPoint document with you. Especially on a windy day like today. I have been on a bit of a crusade for people not to take big documents to meetings because it's easy to spend your time telling clients about the ideas you had before you arrived. Sometimes that's relevant but I think it's often better to listen and enquire and be curious. You can always send the document on later.'

We're through the Royal Botanical Gardens now and sauntering alongside the iconic Sydney Opera House as John explains point two.

'A real advantage of taking to the streets – and this is why I started doing this – is it's a bit more healthy than sitting down, drinking coffee and eating muffins. When you're walking you're expending calories, not consuming them. We have a commitment to balance and mental health, so me doing this in the middle of all the busyness is leading by example.' It's an important point. People follow what leaders do, not what they say. And though John didn't actually refer to 'walking the walk', I knew what he meant.

His third point is the most interesting to me – a real piece of Street Wisdom about the link between physicality and thought.

'Sitting in the office, it's easy to get immersed in the problem – stuck in it. Walking out here gives you a different perspective. You can imagine the problem as an object you've left in the office back there. You can look down or across or up at the problem. Creating a bit of physical distance gives you thinking space.'

We only have forty-five minutes outside but we come back to the office feeling like it's been two hours. The reception area is buzzing, espresso is brewing and John's next meeting is about to begin. 'Now, if you're signing a multi-million-dollar deal or doing a video conference with someone in a different time zone, you would probably want to do that up here. But taking clients for a walk is often less pressure and more relationship focused and clients seem to really like it.'

9

Lost and Found

'All I ever wanted was a world without maps.'
Michael Ondaatje, The English Patient

**New discoveries await us when we leave our routine routes
and head off the well-trodden paths into uncharted
territory. But, to do this we need to risk not knowing
where we are. Let's look at why that's a risk worth taking,
how deliberately choosing to lose your way can be very
creative and why sometimes we need to get lost to find
what we're looking for.**

To be candid, I am not quite sure where we are. Somewhere between page 150 and the end of the book, for sure, but I have been so absorbed in this enjoyable wander with you that I have lost my bearings. Which, makes this the perfect time for a chapter about the power of losing your way to find what you're looking for.

Street Wisdom WalkShops rarely end where they begin, and

often, we won't give participants a precise finishing point until the last minute. This is deliberate. We want them to free themselves from knowing exactly where they are headed and when they are due to arrive. But it makes people nervous – not knowing – and that's deliberate, too. Because a bit of disorientation has proven to be an essential ingredient of the experience.

I should mention that getting lost comes naturally to me; I have an exuberantly faulty sense of direction. I am the person who's guaranteed to turn the wrong way out of my hotel room and end up in the laundry cupboard instead of the lift. Every time. 'Not all those who wander are lost', says Tolkien (in *The Fellowship of the Ring*). True, Mr Tolkien, not *all*. But *some* are, believe me. My talent for wandering off course might explain why I founded a social venture that encourages others to do the same.

Having an on-off relationship with the compass was something of a challenge when I studied to be a pilot. Yes, I'll let that sentence sink in. Me, at the controls of a lethal flying machine – a person who has been described since birth as having his head in the clouds, actually *in the clouds*. But flying was a childhood dream. I used to walk to school imagining I was at the controls of a Spitfire, and I wasn't going to let a wayward direction-finder in my mind get in the way.

On one of my early solo sorties, I was looking to land outside London at Oxford airport. I'd studied the map, plotted the course and faithfully followed the bearing. But there was no sign of Oxford anywhere. I flew in a tight circle for a while, getting more and more uneasy. What you may not know is that the country is covered with a network of specialist radio stations manned by air traffic controllers (many volunteers) who exist to help idiots like me find their way. That doesn't mean my ego would allow me to use them. 'I can find my way', said the voice circling in my head. But the visibility was fading and the fuel needle heading towards the red. With panic rising, I finally caved in, nudged my pride aside and reached for the radio. 'This is Whisky Alpha Charlie Bravo calling Oxford tower. Er... Where do I find you?' I shall never forget the air traffic controller's deadpan response. 'Look down!' I winced at her voice. Turns out I had found Oxford accurately but couldn't see it because I was right on top of it.

HOME SWEET HOMING

In the plane, circling over my destination in the twilight, I wasn't lost. But I *felt* lost, and it wasn't a good feeling. There's a good reason why. To the reptilian, primed-to-survive brain buried inside us, lost means *vulnerable to attack.* Our hunter-gatherer forebears (and remember the human race has been hunter-gatherer for 90 per cent of its history, so no surprise the conditioning is strong) continually roamed large, hostile territories searching for scant food. The nomadic life had its perils, so knowing where the nearest shelter, cave, defensible hilltop was would have been crucial.

It's true our ancestors developed considerable navigational skill, but before we get too self-congratulatory, it should be remembered that our ability to find our way around the Earth is primitive compared to some of the planet's more skilled pathfinders.

The humpback whale can travel over vast oceans without deviating by a single degree. The monarch butterfly migrates, unerringly, thousands of miles from the USA to Mexico every year. Humble starlings have reliably refound their nest from 800km (500 miles) away. But that's routine compared to the Manx shearwater (*Puffinus puffinus*) that was released in Massachusetts and flew 4,900km (3,050 miles) across the Atlantic back to its roost in Britain. Or the equally impressive Laysan albatrosses that have been tracked flying for ten exhausting non-stop days from Whidbey Island near Vancouver to Midway Island, to land accurately on their tiny, blink-and-you'll-miss-it home in the Pacific. What would these superb avian aviators have thought of me circling Oxford blindly in my Cessna 172? The shame!

Knowing our way home – literally *homing* – became especially important with the arrival of the agrarian era, when humans began clustering in villages and farms. These locations now needed cultivating and protecting. Humans suddenly had a definable place that they were 'from', and it was a place you needed to be able to find your way back to.

No sooner did humanity start settling down than it also became more restive. Home, as any teenager will tell you, is the perfect place to run away from. The impulse to explore the wider world was driven by territorial ambitions and the need to trade. That, and plain curiosity. The desire to know what's over 'them thar hills' is an enduring part of the human psyche. Following that curious itch has powered our species' exploration of our planet.

While we humans may not have the on board navigational prowess of the whale, starling or albatross, we had the ingenuity to create a tool to compensate. The map.

CHARTING PROGRESS

It seems for our very first attempts at map-making, early man didn't look down to the Earth, but up to the stars. Small dots scored into the Lascaux Cave paintings around 14,500 BC show our cave-dwelling ancestors signposting the heavens by identifying constellations and prominent stars. Before long, the ancient Babylonians are creating maps on clay tablets and when the ancient Greeks start drawing maps on paper, our new way-finding technology becomes portable. The first extant map of the world was drawn up by the philosopher Anaximander. It would be more appropriate to say the *known* world, because it's essentially a map of Greece, plus some surrounding ocean. But, that's one thing about maps; they don't show us the world, they show how the map-maker sees the world.[1]

Early on, much of the detail was guesswork and hearsay, with large areas left empty except for warning signs: *Here be dragons!* and so on. Region by region, exploration by exploration, we began to fill in the gaps. Progressively, our species extended its knowledge of the Earth, and with it a sense of dominion. Aided by our map-making abilities, we penetrated further and further into the wilderness, bringing 'civilisation' with us. It is worth remembering that the word civilisation derives from the Latin *civitas* (city), and that the march of 'progress' can be tracked in the spread of towns and cities across previously untouched land – and not just land.

Navigation is a nautical term. Charting the seas has enabled us to find our way across vast tracts of open sea to explore, trade and conquer. To make this task more achievable, we started segmenting nautical maps into neat grids of latitude and longitude. Latitude was relatively easy to work out by plotting a

---

1. On a recent trip to Australia, I was intrigued – and shocked – to come across a map that showed the continent richly overlaid with a dazzling variety of interlocking colours. It wasn't an artwork but a representation of the 120 indigenous nations that inhabited the land for countless centuries before colonisers "discovered" Australia in the eighteenth century. Settlers' maps – the ones most of us grew up with – show the entire area an empty, uniform khaki with here and there an anglicised place name. What a perfect pictorial representation of the colonial mindset. You can see a copy of Australia's Aboriginal Map at https://aiatsis.gov.au/.

boat's position against the height of the sun. Longitude was much more challenging and required accurate timing as well as positioning. To plot where you are accurately, you have to know exactly how long it is since you last plotted where you were. Boats needed two clocks: one that told them local time and another telling the time in their port of origin, and both of these clocks needed to be accurate. That's another story and you can read about it in Dava Sobel's gripping book *Longitude*. But the upshot was, in a collective effort to find its way around the planet, humanity had to agree not only to a common map, but a common temporal standard. Our desire to orientate ourselves and *know the unknown* has domesticated not only the planet but Time itself.

That impulse continues to this day. When you consult your smartphone to find out where you are, where you are going and how long it's going to take to get there, you do so thanks to the US government's Global Positioning System. GPS is a network of originally twenty-four (now thirty-one) satellites that the Americans lofted into orbit in 1973 to provide its military with accurate place and time information anywhere on Earth. Civilians were permitted[2] to use it from the 1980s and it was fully operational from 1995. It's taken the map-making instinct in us to a whole new level. Thanks to GPS and technologies, you can now locate yourself pretty much anywhere on the planet. Everest. Guadalajara. Phnom Penh. Upper Volta. Click on your smartphone and you'll know where you are, to within a few metres – and also, to the millisecond, what the time is.

2. I say 'permitted', because access to GPS is in the gift of the US government. Which is why other global powers like Russia and China have been developing their own alternatives.

Undeniably convenient, but also, I feel, something of a shame.

THE LOST ART OF GETTING LOST

Getting lost is unsettling, yes, but also exciting. Even romantic. We know that, because the French have a specific word for that giddy but enchanting disorientation you feel in an unfamiliar place: *dépaysement*. But like many other delights on our turbo-charged Earth, we are in danger of losing it.

Atef Alshehri, an historian and urban architect friend in Saudi Arabia, was telling me recently about how in the cooler winter months his brother heads off into the wilderness of the desert and sets up camp. I was touched to hear that a timeless Bedouin tradition survives modernity. Then he explained what camping in the desert means to his brother in this GPS-enabled age. You jump into a powerful four by four and follow the on board satnav to a predetermined spot where an air-conditioned tent (with fully stocked kitchenette and generator) awaits you. There you while away your day on social media, watching Netflix and duelling each other on PlayStation, and for dinner you dial up a takeaway, which is brought to you, under the starry blackness, by a courier on a souped-up trials bike using Google Maps.

The majestic expanse of the desert, humbled by mobile phone.

'I have always loved the desert. One sits down on a desert sand dune, sees nothing, hears nothing. Yet through the silence something throbs, and gleams...' said Antoine de Saint-Exupéry in *The Little Prince*. Today, that mysterious 'something' is liable to be a courier's bike bringing you a pizza.

The more dependent we allow ourselves to become on navigational aids, the less we rely on our innate navigational skills. And science tells us we're losing what we're not using.

The hippocampus is a seahorse-shaped[3] area of the brain responsible for memory and spatial navigation. Central to our ability to build mental maps, it develops with use, as studies of the brains of London cab drivers have proved. 'Cabbies' go through years of training (they call it The Knowledge), physically criss-crossing the miasma that is Greater London until they have memorised every street. This activity so stimulates the cabbies' brains that their hippocampi are visibly larger than those of non-taxi drivers.

Just as finding your own way around builds the hippocampus, there's now evidence that outsourcing this to technology has the opposite effect. Researchers at McGill University have found people who use GPS have markedly less grey matter and neural functionality than those who don't.[4] The brain is demonstrably less able to navigate. Soon the whole human race may be joining me in the hotel laundry room.

Being more technology-oriented is also making us more isolated.

We discourage the use of smartphones during our Street Wisdom events. This is partly to give participants momentary respite from their incessant emails, but also, off screen, people have to explore. When we ask people to turn their device off, a hand always goes up with an anxious question as to how they will find their way without a navigation app. We often get very sceptical looks back if we suggest they could ask a passerby. People seem to have forgotten a time before smartphones when a local was the go-to source of information. Countless conversations between strangers used to open with 'Can you

3. Hence its name, a combination of the Greek for 'horse' and 'sea-monster'.
4. https://bit.ly/3htFJjk

tell me the way to…?'. Our streets are less friendly, less alive without those conversations.

Street Wisdom has been doing all it can to counter this dehumanising tide of geopositional certainty. Uncomfortable though it may feel initially, experience shows there are many and varied benefits to reacquiring the lost art of being lost. Here are four.

1. Being lost makes us pay attention

It's the tail end of a long day visiting Marrakesh. You've seen the sights and sipped mint tea. You've seriously soukhed. And now it's time to head back to your riad with the family. It's getting late, so that shortcut looks inviting, but only a couple of twists and turns later and you've lost your bearings. One minaret is looking much like another and as you press on, you're beginning to feel more and more – out of place. This is definitely not the tourist trail. Eyes seem to watch impassively from darkened doorways. Your children are holding your hand a little bit tighter. Radiating confidence as best you can, you scan every shop, every street sign for a directional clue. Near tears, one of your children asks, 'Dad, are we lost?' Suddenly, your perceptions go into overdrive. Gone is the holidaying parent, replaced by the instinctive pathfinder. With your perceptions awakened, you're taking in all the details, scouring your surroundings for clues. You're noticing that if the dying sun is to your back, then right is… south.

This is a real memory from a real trip to Morocco.

Thanks to some helpful directions from a passing granny (you see, ask a stranger!) and a lot of sign language, we found our way home in the end, flopping on to our beds with relief and a sense of real achievement. And that's the point. Getting lost can be stressful but it wakes you up. It demands that you pay attention, that you get out of your head and connect with your surroundings. Shaken from your mental routine, you focus on what's really going on.

It wasn't the best experience we had that holiday, but it's our strongest memory. Twenty-five minutes out of seven days, and years later, that's what we remember.

2. Being lost makes us more creative

Actually, I'd say you can't get creative without getting lost. I say that because staring at the laptop screen right now, I am lost. Words come in bursts, but in-between…

There's silence.

I am lost for words, not knowing what comes next. It's like a part of my brain is asking for directions and, hopefully, another part of my mind answers back. Arthur Koestler, who wrote copiously on creativity, put it beautifully when he said: 'Creative activity could be described as a type of learning process where teacher and pupil are located in the same individual.'

When we enjoy something as complete-feeling as a great film, play, song or painting, it is tempting to imagine the work is as the creator originally conceived it, but that's rarely the case. Originators often start with little more than a fragment or impulse. The ensuing twists and turns of the creative process means they are as surprised as we are by what is finally produced.

The creative arts are littered with examples of this productive disorientation.

One of the most re-recorded songs in all popular music is Leonard Cohen's 'Hallelujah'. It's so simple, so natural, so naturally singable you might think it just fell out of Cohen's head and on to the page. In fact, the song we know today, mostly through the haunting recording by Jeff Buckley,[5] actually went through eighty draft versions, each with different tempos, time signatures, keys and lyrics. At one point in the decades-long creative journey, Cohen got so lost, and so frustrated, that he was found sitting in his underwear in New York's Royalton Hotel physically banging his head on the floor.

Not only did Ernest Hemingway try out multiple titles for his masterpiece *A Farewell to Arms* (including 'Love in War', 'World Enough and Time', 'Every Night and All', 'Of Wounds and Other Causes'), he also wrote forty-seven different endings. The book we know today is really a freeze frame of the author's process of searching.

Robert Altman, one of the most accomplished filmmakers of our time, makes no bones about it. 'I am not an expert. That is someone else's job. If I were expert, the approach would be all wrong. It would be from the inside. I am a blunderer. I usually don't know what I am going into at the start. I go into the fog and trust something will be there.'

Most of us avoid that fog of not knowing. Creativity requires us to seek the murk and when we find it, resist the desire to turn the fog lights on. This isn't just tolerating the sensation of being lost, but inviting it and even, eventually, coming to enjoy it, and that takes practice. I know, because I have spent the past few decades practising, not just in the street but also on stage, in front of a paying public.

As I've mentioned, I grew up in the opera world. It's a complex art form with lots of moving parts. It takes large forces to stage and it's ferociously expensive, which is why, though the performances may look wonderfully free, emotional and spontaneous, the process and industry are very controlled and constrained. I love traditional opera but over time I wanted to take away the guard rails and try something more

5. https://bit.ly/3hwYhiK

and unpredictable. Some intrepid colleagues [6] and I effectively threw away the rule book and started exploring what it would be like to make up operas on the spot, without any rehearsal, prepared music or story. In musical terms, that's dense fog.

It sounds scary, and it is. Even after many years performing together, a night on stage with my improvising opera company (Impropera) still has the capacity to terrify. But, I have found the creative payback is more than worth the fear. Indeed, fear is a critical part of jolting my mind out of safety and into real creativity.

The first time I properly stepped into the foggy unknown as a young improviser was because I was too scared not to. The rest of the company had completed a scene and left the stage. I looked around and there was no one to start a new scene – no one but me. I had no choice. But also, I had no ideas.

I hovered, waiting for inspiration, but time was running out and my colleagues were just looking at me, enjoying my creative discomfort as only fellow improvisers can. The cavalry wasn't coming. So I stepped on stage, opened my mouth – and nothing came out.

Nothing. Niente. Nada. Zip.

My mind was a complete blank. 'Don't panic', I told myself as the piano introduction covered my silence. Something will come.

It didn't

And after a while… it still didn't.

At that point my attention, my entire life really, collapsed into what felt like a tunnel of shame. Blood rushed through my ears. I felt truly lost. But then I heard a strange distant sound. Applause. Cheering. Somewhere out there, beyond the foot-

6. Morag McLaren, Susan Bisatt, Niall Ashdown, Peter Furniss and Anthony Ingle

Applause. Cheering. Somewhere out there, beyond the foot-lights, the audience was urging me on. It is something I have seen many times since; the audience loves to see performers dare to get into real trouble. I think it may be because they are so grateful it's not them up there on stage. They – we – all know that nightmarish fear of being in public and not know-ing what comes next, and because of that, I feel the public is full of compassion for idiots like improvisers, who go and stand in that awkward place of not knowing to entertain others.

Encouraged by the clapping and foot-stamping, I blurted out the first words that came into my mind. 'Plastic people, plastic world…' Correction, the words came directly to my vocal cords without any conscious help from me. That's how, when it's good, improvising feels. You don't need to know what comes next, the words appear. You are not singing, you are *being sung*.

That, in my view, is why it's worth putting ourselves through the anxiety of not knowing. The reward for willingly losing your way is that you find things you never would have otherwise.

As Street Wisdom's favourite creativity guru Sir Ken Robin-son puts it: 'If you are not prepared to be wrong, you'll never come up with anything original.' Put it another way, the abil-ity to allow yourself to lose your way – on the stage, on the street, in life – is a prerequisite of creativity.

3. Being lost is liberating

The flamenco tradition has a word they use to describe this extraordinary state when the performers lose themselves in the music and reach a whole new level of presence. 'Duende! Duende!' the audience shouts to signal that the performer has let go of the safety zone of their skill and entered somewhere more mysterious and – yes – magical.

The psychologist Mihaly Csikszentmihalyi coined the word 'flow' to describe this heightened state where you are so absorbed in what you're doing that you effectively disappear into the experience. In the classic movie *The Hustler*, Paul Newman talks about being in 'flow' when he's playing pool. The cue becomes a piece of wood with nerves in it. He explains the feeling as 'a guy knows, he just knows, he feels it, he's got everything working for him… time and touch'.

Not knowing where you are going. Knowing where you are heading but not knowing how you are going to get there is a potent state to put yourself in.

Shamans enter these altered states of consciousness to connect with spirits and retrieve information. The word shaman comes from the Siberian Tungus tribe and means 'one who can see in the dark'. By surrendering themselves to an unknown journey via a rhythmic trance or plant medicine, they can locate wisdom in the spirit realm and trace their way back to the physical world, bringing their secrets with them.

The Chinese have a phrase, 'crossing the river by feeling the stones'. Often used by Deng Xiaoping, it beautifully sums up the experimental, sensitised state you need to be in when you are seeking to find your way through the unknown. You don't think your way across the river, consult a map or squint at your waterlogged smartphone. With bare feet, you *feel* your way, hesitantly, from one hidden underwater foothold to the next, trusting in the truth of your sensations to reach your destination. It's somatic. Trial and error. Responding to what's emerging. Sensitive to the ebb and flow of the environment. True path-finding.

A micro version of that is happening every time you climb a ladder. If you were to film your foot between rungs and slow the film down, you'd see a foot that's lost, free of the rung it has left and seeking for where it thinks the next rung is. Your airborne limb minutely course-corrects its way through the void as it comes into land. We've all experienced the jarring opposite when we trip down a step that we thought wasn't there. Or worse, arrive with a thump at the bottom of some steps when we meet the ground earlier than we expected. Every single step you take is a game of lost and found.

The point is, not knowing where you are, but feeling where you might be, is a heightened state. A while ago in our wander, in *Tuning-In*, we talked about wanting to activate our embodied intelligence. Disorientation is a wonderful way to do that.

4. Being lost is real

Our wanderings through this chapter bring us – as wanderings do – back to where we started, to the idea that *feeling lost* and *being lost* are not the same.

Feeling lost is that uncomfortably queasy sensation that follows when we discover we are not where we thought we were. It contains with it a judgement, a self-criticism: we don't know where we are and we *should*. Being lost is purely a situation. With the judgement taken out, I'd argue it's a situation most of us find ourselves in most of the time.

The human mind spends most of its time interpreting what happened and trying to anticipate what's going to happen. Our interpretation of the past is highly subjective and our ability to accurately predict what's coming is sketchy at best.

Go on, admit it. We don't really know where we were or where we are going. We *are* lost. We paper over this fact by post-justifying our history and setting real-sounding goals for our future, positioning ourselves in terms of past achievements/ relationships and soon-to-be-realised aspirations. Technological trinkets aside, we're not so different from our ancestors, looking up at the heavens wondering which way we're pointing or how long remains on the clock before we arrive at our final, final destination.

So we stay busy. Criss-crossing our world on short-term errands and filling up the days with to-dos so we don't have to contemplate the annoying, puzzling, ultimately terrifying idea that we have no idea where we are. Scary…

Or is it? I have been as hustly-bustly as anyone for a lot of my life but my recent experiences with Street Wisdom have introduced me to the liberating effects of *choosing to be lost.*

When you accept the humbling idea of being lost, the humiliation seems to disappear. It's the difference between a commuter who catches the wrong train by mistake and the adventure-seeker who catches the wrong train on purpose. I've done both. Believe me, there's a difference. One feels like an annoying, time-wasting, nail-biting, embarrassing mistake; the other feels like opening a portal to the unknown.

That's why I designed some time to be lost – productively lost – into Street Wisdom.

It sounds like one of those Taoist paradoxes, but it's been my experience (and the experience of many participants using Street Wisdom to crack a problem that's been on their minds) that when you lose your way, you find a way.

Leanne Wiles shared this story at one of our recent Walk-Shops:

'Interestingly, when being drawn to what I was attracted to, I lost my bearings (in a city I know inside out) and challenged myself to find the way back without using a phone. Which involved stopping busy people to ask for directions. Something I only really do on holiday. It really stood out for me – being uncertain in a place I am normally certain of and having interactions with other people who were rushing around. Getting lost was surprisingly eye-opening.'

That's a common story at Street Wisdom events. When we self-direct less, we allow ourselves to be guided more. People regularly return from a Street Wisdom walk to share tales of how they were nudged to turn this way or that by a sight or a sound, an intriguing object or an attractive stranger. Some describe this guidance in almost mystical terms:

'To my surprise I was also drawn to the sounds of birds and that of the murky Thames' water lapping on the rugged, stony riverbank. When asked to slow right down and observe the world from that place, I noticed how I had never seen so much peace and joy in the people passing by. Thinking back, I wonder if it was because of the calmness and peace I felt within as I let time stand still...'

Others are more pragmatic:

'I am not sure how it happened, but somehow during the event I came back to myself and started seeing the world more gently and kindly.'

But the sense of guidance is palpable.

Many of them are seeking answers for the questions on their minds. In some cases, these are intractable problems they have been wrestling with for months, even years. These are not lost souls, but the answers they are seeking seem to have eluded them. And oddly, mindfully wandering around for a couple of hours helps them trip over the answer.

It's something we'd encourage you to experience for yourself in a Street Wisdom workshop, but here's a little exercise you can try in the meanwhile.

EXERCISE: LET'S GET PRODUCTIVELY LOST

What?

A short experience that helps you feel more comfortable with the idea of being lost.

Why?

Being lost can be a freeing, mind-opening experience. But for reasons of survival, it's an experience our minds are hardwired to protect us from. It's not only dangerous to be lost, it's also embarrassing. I say that as an English male and we'd normally prefer the former to the latter. It's why I will keep reassuring my wife I know where I am driving, long, long after we both know that's not true.

To get productively lost, you'll have to get comfortable with being vulnerable, admitting you don't know where you are, relying on others for guidance. This exercise helps you practise. Warning: It's simple to describe but can be exquisitely uncomfortable to do.

How?

Go to an obvious landmark in a part of a town you know well. Stand with your back to it and ask strangers: 'Can you tell me the way to [landmark]?'

You are probably going to feel silly doing this. Your brain is going to resist pretending not to know something it does know, but keep at it. You are taming the egoic, know-it-all part of yourself. It's the inner direction setting that is keeping you safely 'on track' but preventing you from discovering the treasures and delights you might find in a wrong turning.

Asking directions is also a great exercise to help reach across the space between yourself and a passer-by. If we were to practise it more, it would make our cities more friendly, our towns more alive. And being lost – or choosing to pretend to be – is a great way to start.

You can see a digital version of this exercise here: streetwisdom.org/wanderful-exercises/

MEET A STRANGER — ESPERIDE

The sun is up in a pure, cold Italian sky and Esperide is not just wandering with me but also wondering.

'What is everyone doing here?'

It's Sunday morning. The town of Ivrea would normally be practically empty. Yet today it's jammed with people and proving impossible to park. Both of us are wondering if we should have gone to Milan instead of following our intuition and opting for the far less well-known but usually less crowded town of Ivrea.

We needn't have worried. It may be the weekend, but synchronicity is definitely at work.

Having jammed the hire car between a delivery van and a recycling bin and parking Italian-style, we find ourselves standing at a corner, debating which way to head into town. On the wall in front is a poster of a man dressed as Black Panther. The headline is a single word – *arruolamento*!

And the penny drops.

Every year, Ivrea hosts an epic food fight called The Battle of the Oranges. It involves the townspeople togging up in medieval armour and pelting each other with tons of oranges – and I mean pelting, really clobbering – from the rooftops and with catapults. The organisers say if you don't want to get hit, you can wear a red beanie hat that signifies you're a non-combatant, but don't believe it. Everyone gets whacked at some point as the streets pile up knee-deep in orange peel. The interesting by-product of this fruit frenzy is surprisingly high levels of social cohesion in the town. Evidently, if you give people a chance to exorcise their irritations one week a year, they can live more harmoniously with each other for the remaining fifty-one.

This citric punch-up is held to mark Carnivale [in February] and today's the early January day when the different factions, including Black Panthers, drum up support [you can hear the drums and singing in the distance] and try to get people to enrol in their teams of extravagantly costumed orange hurlers or *aranceri*.

The *Pantera negra* in the poster dares us to sign up. Last time I attended the battle I got splatted by a high-velocity orange and I have to say the idea of revenge is tempting.

We're about to head off when Esperide points out another, smaller sign, which reminds us that the spot where we are standing is on the path of the Via Francigena, the ancient pilgrimage route that runs from Canterbury to Rome.

I can't help noticing that in the first moments of our wander, without taking a step, we've already stumbled over many elements that I associate with Esperide. Italy, food, festivity, animals [her name is a species of butterfly], international connections [she speaks seven languages], a mixture of contemporary and the ancient, fun and the sacred. She's also something of a superhero, today less Black Panther and more Catwoman, in her fake-fur leopard-skin trench coat, black top, white scarf and glittery gold handbag. As she will explain later, the brightly coloured clothing is a mindful choice.

Esperide lives and works in a celebrated eco-community in the Italian Alps called Damanhur. Sited in the nearby valley of Valchiusella, it's an extraordinary place, a creative incubator for social, spiritual and sustainable development that I've been visiting for inspiration and pleasure for over two decades. So today I am returning to a place where the seeds of Street Wisdom were first planted, and to meet up with someone who was instrumental in planting them.

As we head into town, pressing through the boisterous crowds, Esperide reminds me that the roots of innovation go deep in Ivrea thanks to its most famous son, the socially minded Adriano Olivetti.

'He built the company with a strong sense of meaning, doing something good for the community, not just making money.

193

Everybody around here used to work for Olivetti. There was such a sense of trust that people didn't need cash in the shops if they didn't have it. Everyone knew they'd get paid.'

We pause by the bridge and look up the valley to the snow-capped foothills of the Alps...

'Olivetti understood the importance of keeping your roots with the land so rather than drag his workforce into town he created factories up in the villages around Ivrea where people could work. Most were organised as cooperatives. He saw there were rural communities here and he said we should respect them. He also understood how important it was to empower women. The place I work now was once an Olivetti plant where women made the typewriter cases.

'When he died, his heirs thought this socially minded approach was not cost-effective so they closed everything. People that want-ed to work for them had to move and that was the end of any form of economic life in these valleys. It was a real shame, but on the other hand, our valleys have been kept relatively pristine. No non-organic farming and little exploitation. So today it's really beautiful.'

Though she spends a lot of time in the countryside, Esperide is a city girl at heart.

'I grew up in Milan and I love cities, particularly big cities like New York. I love the people, the diversity, the busyness. Feeling you are at the centre of the world. What I don't like in cities any more is how hard it is to breathe. After living many years in a place like this, I find the polluted air a real stretch.

'Also, there is a thing I can't bear in these big cities – that everyone dresses in black. I understand why they want to do this. It's like wrap-ping yourself in insulation foil. On the other hand, you lose contact with the little life there might be in the environment around you.'

194

As Esperide speaks, *aranceri* teams in bright yellow, orange, green and blue are thronging past. I spot members of the Ace of Spades [*Asso di Picche*] team, the Devils and the Chess [*Scacchi*] squad. The style could perhaps be described as dayglo-Renaissance.

'At Damanhur we like to think about how different colours might resonate with the energy and symbology of different days of the week. And how you might choose to be in tune with those energies by wearing those colours. So Monday – moon day – you might want to wear white, silver, light blue... colours associated with the lunar. Sunday is associated with the sun and I like to wear a whole range of different colours because the sun gives life to everything. So Sunday is really great...'

Ah, now I understand the sequinned handbag! A group of faux Napoleonic soldiers walk past, eyed with indulgence by a couple of real Carabinieri, and a witch.

A witch?

This weekend is doubly significant as it's Epiphany, the day Italian children get visited by a candy-toting witch called the Befana. You get sweets if you've been good but a sock full of coal [actually caramel-covered rock candy] if you've misbehaved during the year. It's a festive tradition with a dark past.

'Literally millions of witches – I just think of them as wise women – were persecuted and killed. Burned at the stake. People think this happened in the Middle Ages but actually it was more during the Renaissance. In the medieval period the connection with the ancient traditions and the elements was still alive. People were living in a mystical reality. With the Renaissance, wisdom became more about the preserve of men. Women who had knowledge of how to heal people with herbs, could help deliver children or had a vision of some kind were regarded as a threat and murdered wholesale. It's a question worth asking: how can a culture blossom in the arts and sciences and at the same time oppress half of the population in this way? We are still living a bit in this dichotomy.'

We've turned into the cobble-stoned road up to the main square.

'Oh look, there's Death!' Esperide points out with delight.

No, it's not a hallucination. We have just happened on another of the *aranceri* recruiting stations – this time for the *Morte* group. With their lurid skull and crossbones logo, they are clearly not taking any hostages! Carnivale is obviously going to be full-on this year. But Ivrea does this for a reason.

Everyone has licence to go crazy for three days. That's exactly the function of carnival. In the Middle Ages, people used to bring donkeys into church to give sermons. Three days of complete chaos, which make it possible to live in an orderly way the rest of the year.

Ivrea, with its usually low crime rate and high social cohesion, bears witness to the power of authorised misrule.

'Each team has its own flag and colour. They compete and fight. But in the end what they all care about is their town. Collectively. We can't deny that humans have competition in them. I don't think we should eliminate it, but use it in an intelligent way – to create more community.'

We battle through the crowds into the central square as Esperide explains a narrative that plays out during the battle of the oranges. It's actually a conflation of two stories. The first harks back to a time during the Middle Ages when the law of *jus primae noctis* meant that local landowners could sleep with any girl of their choice on their wedding night. Then one day a feisty miller's daughter decided enough was enough and cut a noble's throat!

'The orange juice is supposed to remind us of the blood flowing. It also does a great job of cleaning the streets.'

196

David Pearl

This early feminist tale makes me curious about the power of women in Italy. Certainly, as I look around there's hefty amounts of testosterone pumping through the bands of young men braying and waving their team's flag. But, among them are girls who are more than holding their own. And as ever, in Italy, keeping up a steady banter with the males.

'Italian men and women like to flirt. And we know it's just flirting. If a man comes up in the street and tells you you are the most beautiful woman, you want to be with me tonight, you just laugh because you know he is going to do it to the next beautiful woman too. No one gets offended. It's the play of polarity.

'There's a common idea currently that harmony means everyone has to be the same. I think harmony is created by the opposite: by exalting the differences and finding a way they can all coexist. It creates more tension and that means more creativity, more fun and more expression. I think we need to get out of thinking white is better than black or blue is better than green or orange. There's a place for all colours. How can they all coexist by being the best possible version of their own hue?'

As if to agree, three limber Italian cyclists flash by in eye-hurting peacock blue and crimson. They are fit, good-looking and effortlessly jealousy-making.

'I think that Italy is one of those countries where the culture of beauty is very very deep. In everything. In art and design. We understand the value of beauty and the power of beautifying – in elevating the frequency of everyday things. Also, in Italy I feel women unconsciously understand that your beauty is a gift to others. Italian men are very generous with compliments. This is nice because it generates a dynamic where some of our sensual forces can play out without needing to become sexual.

'In other countries I visited, there is probably more sex but less sensuality. But what really feeds us here is sensuality, which means also being able to enjoy food and a good glass of wine. Again, in Italy this is all intertwined.

'I think in general if Western countries were to relax a little and not be so focused on sex but start to bring back the joy and the pleasure that our senses can give to life, then everybody would be happier. So many interactions could become softer if we found a space for these energies to play. And then there would be less assault, which is currently a huge problem. If we don't transform our awareness, take responsibility to be the best we can, commit to growing together – men and women – we will all continue to suffer.'

Esperide says all this with a combination of seriousness and hu-mour. A hallmark of the work I have seen her do with organisations and their leaders around the world.

'People talk about having new vision. How can you do that if your senses are closed? The physical senses translate the reality outside of us. If we constantly limit the amount of stimuli, we have less and less of a basis for intuition insight. Leaders need to be able to feel, perceive and read other people. This is not something you can learn on a diagram or PowerPoint. You learn it by developing your senses, by feeling the energy of the other person so you know who you are talking to. People are not machines.'

We're heading out of the ancient heart of the town, back to the car and modern life. It feels like I've been time-travelling – another hallmark of time spent with Esperide, and it prompts me to ask my final question: if Esperide could live in any period of history, when would she choose?

'I would choose somewhere in the future.'

I am surprised by her answer as many people are pretty fright-ened about the future.

David Pearl

'Yes, but I am imagining a wonderful future...'

10

The Wisdom of Strangers

'There are no strangers here; only friends you haven't met yet'
William Butler Yeats

Our fear of strangers has deep roots. But, as we've discovered over time in Street Wisdom, when we stop ignoring and/or fearing others, start sharing what's on our minds and asking for guidance, we discover strangers can be great teachers.

'Cheeeldren. Where are you?' coos the creepy, gimlet-eyed man with a ferret nose and an undertaker's top hat festooned with dusty, dead flowers. He's a vision of nightmares and he's looking straight at me.

One of the most terrifying moments of my young life was meeting the Child Catcher in Chitty Chitty Bang Bang. Yes, it was a virtual encounter – him on screen, me cowering behind my parents in a darkened cinema – but the terror felt absolutely real.

'My little mice, come to me'. The pest exterminator disguised as children's entertainer is dangling lollipops from his skeletal fingers to tempt the town's children out of hiding, I will them not to but they fall into the trap. As the cage door clangs shut, a powerful piece of early learning clicks into place: don't trust strangers!

Through the ages, adults have sought to teach children valuable life lessons through cautionary tales. There's something about a story (particularly one that scares the bejaysus out of a kid) that helps burn the lesson in the memory. One of the essential lessons that parents want us to learn in our young lives is this: if a smiley old man in a moth-eaten top hat offers you sweeties – RUN!

It's not unreasonable. There are predators out there and we need to be aware of them. Stranger Danger – a phrase that arose in the wake of a rash of child abductions in the 1970s and 80s – is real, but not anywhere near as widespread[1] as its champions used to claim.

And yet there's another story, one that most of us live most days. In this story, strangers aren't a menace. They are no stranger than we are. They are the people we pass on the street and sit next to on the bus. Thousands of them. They are just people like us who we haven't met yet. At Street Wisdom, we've been exploring this alternative story and discovering that 'those people' we spend time avoiding eye contact with and dodging on the pavement are usually a lot less frightening than we've been taught to believe; sometimes they can even be valuable guides on our journey.

1. As researchers like Elizabeth Jeglic, Ph.D. (author of Protecting Your Child from Sexual Abuse) point out, '93 per cent of sexual abuse against children is perpetrated by those known to the child'. Danger derives not so much from strangers we don't know but from the strangeness that may lurk within those we think we do.

LONELY CROWDS

Step on to the street with me. It could be anywhere from Reading to Reykjavik. Any time of the day. And one thing you'll notice is there's no shortage of strangers. We're surrounded by people, yet in an odd way we're completely alone. Our cities have never been so crammed, yet loneliness is at epidemic proportions.

A recent BBC survey[2] revealed that a full third of the (55,000) respondents often have feelings of loneliness. That picture is mirrored in bustling metropolises around the world. This is relatively new. The word loneliness didn't even exist before 1800, when people generally used to live in smaller, more connected communities where everyone knew everyone else's business. There was less privacy, perhaps, but much more connection.

The ebbing away of communities has been accompanied by a rise in individualism. An elbows-out, each-person-for-themselves attitude may be a helpful tactic for getting ahead in our capitalistic world, but it is corrosive for societies, undermining our ability to connect to each other.

Nor is so-called success (if we can ever attain it) any antidote to isolation. On the contrary, the fame and fortune we are continually encouraged to seek intensifies the problem. In their book *Affluenza: When Too Much is Never Enough*, Clive Hamilton and Richard Denniss make a very strong case that 'selfish capitalism' and 'luxury fever' is making us unhappier, unhealthier and more alienated. One poignant example of this is the super-successful, globe-trotting international trader I knew of who, having miraculously survived a serious car crash, took out

2. https://bbc.in/3hzzlHt

her phone and realised she had no one to call to share the good news with.

There are many movements now trying to re-knit our communities and answer our desire for connection. Across the world we are seeing *Smile at a Stranger* campaigns and people handing out *I Talk to Strangers* buttons. One community-catalysing organisation we've worked closely with is the British-based but internationally active 'secular church' Sunday Assembly. It was set up by founders Pippa Evans and Sanderson Jones for people who aren't looking for religion but who do miss the regular interconnection with others that going to church used to provide.

Connecting strangers wasn't the central purpose of Street Wisdom, but over time that has emerged as an unexpected benefit of the work we do on the streets. While there's absolutely no pressure for participants to talk to a stranger, it is something we warmly encourage.

First, it's enjoyable.

In her book, *When Strangers Meet,* the activist author Kio Stark argues persuasively in favour of the 'exquisite interruptions' of having even a brief conversation on the street with someone you don't know. Encouraging 'fleeting intimacy' with strangers and enjoying the 'shimmer of connection' that it generates isn't just good for society, it's good for us too.

Also, it knits us together.

Consider Minnie, one of our highly creative Street Leaders. She kicked off a Street Wisdom experiment in an old covered market by holding up a scribbled sign – 'Free Conversation' – and simply waiting. For a while nothing happened. The offer may have seemed too open and generous to the average reserved Brit, but then three elderly men approached her – elderly but, to Minnie, at first glance rather menacing. Broken noses, scarred hands, but no, they weren't ageing gangsters.

They were market traders who had worked on the site many years before it was turned into the trendy shopping destination it is today, and they wanted to talk, to share their memories and laugh about old stories. Everyone enjoyed this moment of fleeting intimacy. Stories are an essential part of our social fabric, reminding us who we are, how we got here and what went before. Passing on oral history, even in this light-hearted way, helps maintain that fabric.

But most importantly, we can learn a lot from connecting with strangers. *Answers are everywhere*, we like to say, *and so are teachers.*

STRANGER AS GUIDE

The helpful guide is an archetype, a shape-shifting character that has been popping up to offer directions in fairy tales and stories since we started telling them: a frog on a lily pad asking a riddle-like question, an enigmatic 'local' fellow at a crossroads advising which path to take, or warning which not to. The ghostly poet Virgil provided this supernatural roadside assistance when he steered Dante through the twists and turns of hell in the *Inferno*. Tolkien's Gandalf had similarly helpful nudges for Bilbo Baggins; the Scarecrow did it for Dorothy; Tinkerbell for Peter Pan; Jiminy Cricket[3] for Pinocchio and Yoda for Luke Skywalker.

In *The Hero With a Thousand Faces*, Joseph Campbell consolidates world mythology into a kind of grand, unified myth of myths, the Hero's Journey, which describes how humans – troubled, ambitious, curious – set off from the world we know

3. I understand that Jiminy Cricket is a euphemism for Jesus Christ. If true, it would be an entirely appropriate reference to heavenly guidance.

into the unknown in search of solutions and resolutions. The first encounter of the hero journey is with a protective figure (often a little old crone or old man) who provides the adventurer with amulets against the dragon forces he is about to pass. What such a figure represents is the benign, protecting power of destiny. Street Wisdom is, for many, a mini hero's journey: a voyage into the unknown in search of answers. Especially relevant, I think, is Campbell's three-word summary of what the Hero's Journey teaches us – 'follow your bliss'. In one way or another, that's the essential question Street Wisdom participants are asking – how do I better orientate myself towards what brings me joy, satisfaction and – yes – bliss.

'Yes, but what's the point of asking for guidance from someone who doesn't know anything about me?'

It's a question we often hear when we encourage Street Wisdom participants to get a complete stranger's perspective on a question they are wrestling with. Actually, that *is* the point. When we want guidance in life, it would seem to make sense to consult family, friends and colleagues, but their familiarity with us can easily skew their responses. Can they say what they mean without hurting our feelings? Should they tell us what we want to hear or need to hear? And what if the change we're contemplating (be it professional or personal) affects them? Can they set their own interests aside and give us a truly unvarnished answer? The beauty of the strangers we bump into in the street is that we are also strangers to them. And precisely because they *don't* know us and have no axe to grind, they can be dispassionate, objective and straightforward.

I remember well a WalkShop we were running in London for the Israeli-Palestinian peace-making charity, Seeds of Peace. One participant, a Palestinian PR specialist, was stopped on her quest by someone trying to sell her a London bus tour. 'I'll talk to you,' she said, 'provided at the end I can ask you a question.' 'A question about me?' asked the bus guy, caught off guard by the role reversal. 'No, about me and my work in Ramallah,' she replied. No one could have known this, but the bus driver had a real interest in the Middle East and, while no expert, was surprisingly well informed. He wasn't close to the detail but what he said to her went straight to the heart of the topic: 'Stop talking about Israelis, start talking about Palestinians!' She told me afterwards that this simple phrase – shifting the emphasis from complaint to celebration – upended a lot of her thinking about her role and how to perform it more effectively.

Very often, far too often for it to be pure coincidence, guides know a lot more than you think they do. They come in many shapes and sizes. Here are just a few to look out for.

The unexpected expert

My friend Chris is a practised user of Street Wisdom. That doesn't mean he isn't regularly surprised by the experiences he has. One day he was asking two related questions: 'How can I better manage the peaks and troughs in my work?' and 'How can I save more money from the jobs I do get?' He found himself at a bus stop and thought he'd ask a complete stranger. The man he asked smiled and gave him a remarkably precise, well-informed answer. It turns out those were two subjects – workflow and financial management – he teaches at a university course for creatives in London.

Closer to home, my wife, Jo, was trying to figure out how to help raise more money for our kids' school. She'd helped with the book sale and puffed her way through the parent and teachers' 5k run. But how to generate more significant funds with less effort? This was the question she chose to ask when she headed off to one of our WalkShops on a rainy Sunday afternoon. The streets were empty and the few pedestrians she did see had their heads down, hurrying to get out of the rain. Then, in a park, she spotted a middle-aged couple dressed in wet-weather gear and apparently enjoying the downpour. She asked them to pause and posed her question. Good choice. The husband revealed he was a school governor and the wife, a professional head of fundraising.

The hidden teacher

Shilpa, an executive coach based in Delhi, set out on her Street Wisdom quest challenging herself to learn a new skill. Even I thought this was a tall order. To set the scene, we were holding the WalkShop in Karnki, a village in rural Haryana. The villagers seemed pretty suspicious of these obvious outsiders. Also, time was short and Shilpa had only thirty minutes to complete her quest. But off she went, her senses tuned up and willing herself to be open to what the street had to teach. Once the locals had reassured themselves we were not from the government, they warmed to us and began to invite the participants into their shops and homes. One small boy reached out and, without asking, took Shilpa's hand. He led her through an alley into a workshop where his father and brothers were crafting vases from glass. Shilpa expected a hard sell, but, proud of their trade and somehow sensing she was curious, the boy actually wanted to teach her how the glass was made. He even insisted she try blowing a vase herself. Mentors don't just talk, they teach.

During a business event we were running for the employees of the sustainable cosmetics company Lush, a store manager was mulling over the possibility of returning to higher education. Should he? What subject? And how could he organise it? He took these questions out on to the street where he bumped into his old college professor. They sat briefly at a cafe and a couple of mugs of tea later, he had his answers.

The mentor

Google is an organisation that understands the need for continual inspiration. Every year they hold a Summerfest around the world to stimulate, provoke, entertain and inspire the folk who work there. A few years back, Street Wisdom was part of Google's Summerfest in Holland. I was leading the event and noticed a bystander on a bench paying close attention to us. Once I'd sent the participants off on their Quest, I crossed the road and introduced myself. Alpha Sesay had quite a story to tell. Many years before, he had an accident driving home from his own riotous birthday party in Sierra and severely damaged his spine. This awoke him to the plight of other badly injured people in Africa and he helped set up a non-profit (AfricaSurgery.nl) to find them the support they desperately need. But what about Sesay's own health? Doctors told him he would never walk again, but after a decade in a wheelchair he took a closer look at the drugs he was being prescribed, set them aside and decided to try to walk. At his first attempt he managed to totter from his nearby front door to that bench; now he walks 14km (8.6 miles) every day. I asked him to share his story with the inspiration-hunting participants when they returned. It was like Alpha was mentoring us all, giving a living example of how we could each take the next steps in our own journeys. The Summerfesters thanked him, but Alpha insisted he owed his thanks to them. Why? Because he had researched his drugs through Google and it was there he'd discovered their harmful side effects. 'Google is the reason I am walking today.' Inspiring.

Magical friends

These guides are not really strangers at all. They're people you know but don't expect to meet; you find them synchronistically on your path just when you need to hear from them.

London: Back in 2014, Scott was successful but frustrated. The marketing director of a hip, world-famous apparel brand, he was itchy to start his own corporate coaching business but was hesitating. 'Shall I jump now or stay miserable for a bit longer?' was the question he brought to one of the very first Street Wisdom WalkShops we ran in London. He knows the city well, but the tune-up left him a little disorientated. Remember, it's designed to do this so you can see the familiar through fresh eyes. Consequently, he was surprised to find himself on Carnaby Street, a fashion destination where he'd worked many years before. There he met not one, not two but *three* old friends, none of whom he'd seen for ages. And they all asked him the same question. 'Scott, have you set up that new business you were always talking about yet?' Three old friends in an hour, one of whom was living in Australia and only happened to be in Carnaby Street on a whim. Scott got the message, put in his notice and now runs Boom!, a successful agency that shakes businesses out of old thinking.

Copenhagen: Mothers-in-law may not always be classed as friends but when urban planner Just went off on a Street Wisdom Quest to ask if this was the time to build the boat he'd always dreamed of, it was his girlfriend's mother he bumped into unexpectedly. She didn't live in the city and they hadn't seen each other for six months. The first thing she said was, 'Isn't it about time you built that boat…?'

Paris: Hamdi is a senior executive in a Paris-based bank, which had asked us to run a Street Wisdom WalkShop as part of their executive development. Jolly on the surface, there was something strained about him and I made sure we chatted as we walked down to the Champs-Élysées where our WalkShop was to start.

'What's your favourite street in the world and why?' I asked him. It is a question we often use to prime the participants' imagination. He described a curving promenade along the coast outside Tunis where, three decades ago, he and his six-teen-year-old mates used to hang out. The question he wanted to ask on the rues of Paris was: 'How do I make friends in this organisation?' He wasn't friendless exactly but did feel some-thing of an outsider and found it difficult both to attract and retain talent in his department. Hamdi, as I said, comes across as a light-hearted guy and seemed to treat the Street Wisdom experience quite flippantly. When he returned from his quest, apparently 'nothing interesting had happened'. On a hunch, I asked if he'd *met* anyone interesting? And the story came out. Hamdi had bumped into an old friend from Tunisia. Some-one he hadn't seen for thirty years; one of the gang of friends that used to play together on that curving seafront. Hamdi had spent fifteen minutes talking with his buddy, reminiscing about the past and exchanging updated contact details before returning to our business event. 'Don't be a stranger' shouted his re-found friend in parting. 'Stay in touch.' I don't think Hamdi had made a connection between this random meeting and his friendship-related question until that moment. When he realised this long-lost friend might actually *be* telling him the answer to his question, he continued to smile, but was lost for words.

WHEN THE STRANGER IS YOU

I'd like to finish this wander through the subject of strangers with a small, but powerful, personal experience I had when writing this book – actually, this very chapter. About fourteen lines back, I got stuck. Somewhere in the Paris story, the text turned to word salad and I just couldn't say clearly what I wanted to.

When this happens, I'll often go off for a wander to let my mind cool down. Instead of thinking about what I want to say, I'll try to listen to what the book wants me to say.

I decided to wander on my bicycle. Who said you can't wander on two wheels? I had no major plans but found myself pedalling around Regent's Park Outer Circle, a route loved by cyclists as the traffic is restricted and the scenery restful. I was thinking about this chapter and suddenly a phrase came into my mind, one I had heard a progressive US politician, Beto O'Rourke, use in response to an interviewer's question about why he is positive about what he calls 'the genius of immigration'. The phrase was 'we see ourselves in one another' and because I wanted to remember it, I pulled my bike into a driveway, leaned on the handlebars and started making notes on my phone.

'Are you alright?' I hear someone ask and turn to see a British policeman opening a gate and walking towards me. I assure him I am fine and carry on writing. Then I realise there are three policemen. They are not going away. And they are carrying machine guns. These cops are not concerned if I am alright, they are telling me *all is not right*.

As I look around, I realise the gate I have paused in front of leads to the London residence of the US Ambassador. These policemen aren't concerned with my welfare, but they are with his.

I accept I might look strange on my bike. Proper cyclists are normally short, compact types with lightweight physiques and legs bulging like athletic frogs. My nearly two-metre frame is not one you'd immediately stick on a bike. So strange, yes, but a threat? Really? Feeling more unwelcome by the second, I cycle off. As I pass the mosque (ironic, given the fraught geopolitical 'othering' that's going on at the time of writing, that the US Ambassador and London's most prominent Islamic landmark are neighbours), I notice I am being shadowed by a patrol car. Lord knows what would be happening now if I 'looked Muslim'.

Later in the ride, I pause again, wheezing. I blame London's air but in truth it might be lack of fitness. Again I pull to the side of the road. Again I am hunched over the handlebars, and again someone asks:

'Are you alright?'

On edge now, I look up, expecting a gun barrel, but it is a charming old gent who has left his impatient wife at the corner and walked down the road to check on me. He looks like someone who has cycled in the past, has noted me puffing on an inhaler and is genuinely concerned that I might be having an asthma attack or something.

I am touched, reassure him and cycle off. As I pedal home through a beautiful spring morning, I reflect on two starkly contrasting experiences of what it's like to be a stranger. In both cases I am the same person, on the same bike in the same position. The policeman sees someone who may be a danger. The pedestrian sees someone who may be *in* danger.

The way we see strangers is a combination of what we are seeing and the story we tell ourselves about what we are seeing.

That's why, if you remember, in the tuning-up phase for Street Wisdom, we encourage people to 'be drawn to what attracts you *and notice what doesn't*'. This second half of the instruction is designed to make us aware of the judgements we make about the world around us. We will always make those judgements but it's helpful to be aware of the process so uncon-scious assumptions don't affect our behaviour to others without us realising.

I don't blame the policemen, by the way. They are paid to be vigilant.

It's a word I look up when I get home. It has benign enough roots. *Vigil* is associated with reflection and prayer. But as I read on through the definitions, I see *vigilance* (keeping careful watch for danger) and arrive finally at *vigilante*, 'someone who protects, with violence, the interests of an organisation or group that feels threatened'. Watchfulness morphing to violent defensiveness. It reminds me that when we encounter strangers, we have a whole range of responses to choose from, ranging from *welcome* all the way to *war*. We can and should be *alert* about strangers but we don't have to be *alarmed* – what-ever our parents, teachers, newspapers and politicians may tell us. Instead of 'othering', we can opt for empathy, focusing not on how we're different but how we are the same. We can indeed choose to 'see ourselves in others', and hopefully when we are the Stranger, others will do the same for us.

EXERCISE: I AM YOU

Why?

An unexpected benefit of Street Wisdom has been to nudge strangers to connect across the space that divides them and so make our cities warmer, friendlier places. Here is a very simple exercise that I find really helps me open up to feeling more connected with others.

What?

It's fun to be you, yes – but why not try being other people too? This exercise is designed to strengthen your empathy with others, lessen any suspicion of strangers and expand your sense of yourself.

How?

You're walking down the street and a stranger approaches you from the opposite direction. As they approach, look at them without judgement and simply repeat to yourself several times 'I Am You'. Feel the connectedness grow and at the moment you pass each other, imagine your mind (self, soul, spirit, being, operating system… whatever you want to call the part of you that identifies as *you*) jumping from your body into theirs. It's like your being has changed trains and for a few steps imagine you are now literally them. After a few steps riding in someone else's body, you will likely ping back into your own, so keep trying with other passers-by. It will cultivate a sense of connection with others and that we are more alike than different.

You can see a digital version of this exercise here: streetwisdom.org/wanderful-exercises/

'Whenever I come here, I make sure I polish my shoes and wear matching socks.'

Nikita and I are strolling along a spotless pavement, past luminous green topiary bushes that look as if they have been planted by robot. Security guards eye us as we pass. The CCTV cameras watch impassively. Welcome to Canary Wharf, the financial district of towering steel and glass that sprang up in London's docklands in the 1990s.

'This is a bastion of willpower, a triumph of business order over chaos. Everything here says conscientiousness, from the construction of the buildings to the way people dress.'

When Nikita talks about conscientiousness, he's referring to one of the 'big five' personality traits that psychologists, particularly business psychologists like him, use to assess their clients and help them assess themselves.

'Personally, I score very high on neuroticism and extraversion, so my mood goes up and down quick – like the British weather. I'm also high on openness, so life's all very interesting to me. That's probably why I was drawn to psychology in the first place. I am low on agreeableness, so I don't really play nice with others. And really low on conscientiousness. I have about forty-five minutes of willpower a day so I really need to be selective in how I use it. I class myself as completely unemployable, that's why I am a consultant.'

Describing himself with intentional irony as a 'psychonaut', Nikita is something of an expert in psychometrics, helping executives and organisations understand themselves better by scientifically measuring the mysteries of the psyche, but he holds the topic lightly.

'Psychometrics are a tool. It all depends how you use them, I think it's important to treat the whole thing playfully and remember the individual is more important rather than assessment. Let's 'be honest, when you sit in a one-to-one debrief with a person or team to review results, 80 per cent of the value is in creating the space – that hour when there's time to reflect and finish their thoughts. The tool you use as a pretext for this is not halfway as important as the experience itself.'

Which brings us back to footwear.

'Normally, I intentionally mismatch my socks, using a similar pattern but different colours: order and chaos. If people point it out, I'll say "you noticed, you must be highly evidence based".'

So even socks are a psychometric?

'Everything is. People often talk about personality as something that can only be exposed by some test. It's everywhere. We *are* our personality. In the way we act, dress, talk... what we see as meaningful.

'I am personally not that interested in absolutes like introvert and extrovert. I am curious about relativity. For instance, are you more extrovert than your partner? If so, how do you select date night?'

When I push him to define his own relationship, he laughs.

'It's psychological. Olga is logical and I am the psycho!'

We're leaving the squeaky clean, corporate orderliness of Canary Wharf and entering something decidedly murkier. London's Docklands have been tidied up and somewhat gentrified but for centuries this bank of the Thames was home to smugglers, pirates and thieves.

'People are so determined and conscientious – particularly in a place like we have just left – that everything has to have a reason and an ROI [return on investment]. You have to justify why you are doing this or that. So people's range of interest is becoming narrower. Narrower still with cuts in school budgets, arts, sports. Kids are not taken to museums or field trips or opera. Parents are too busy. They might have a predisposition for the arts but never have an exposure to it. They enter a corporate career and have an inkling at the back of their mind of something that really interests them but they cannot justify it, so they go unfulfilled. Over time people can find themselves asking, what am I doing this for – or even why go on living? It can be quite dangerous. They don't have space to explore because work fills all their time.

'I think Jung said it perfectly: what interests you is your future self trying to manifest in the present moment.'

We take a sudden turn to the left down a tiny corkscrewing alley. It's a deliberate move from Nikita.

'We are goal-oriented creatures. When we walk, our eyes are pointing forward and – like in archery – we like to hit the target. When you're walking from A to B it's hard to deviate. So let's deviate!'

Signs tell us that we're on the Thames Path. It's not a route I know. Like most Londoners, if I wanted to get from Canary Wharf to London Bridge, I'd hop on a Tube or jump In a cab. Nikita walks, and he has good psychological reasons for this.

'One of the faults I have is novelty bias so I will sometimes put six, five meetings in a day. Took me quite a while to learn less is more. So now I schedule three meetings in a day and I am a happy man. I leave one to one and a half hours between each meeting so I can plan them on a walking route.'

And this is one of his favourites, winding between refurbished Victorian warehouses, Georgian dwellings, ancient churches, the occasional brutalist 1960s' concrete slab – and pubs. Nikita loves pubs.

'I find cafes too transactional. You buy, you drink, you leave. In a pub, you get a pint – it can be soda water if you wish – and you can take as long as you want. You can loiter. I love that. Also, I like that every pub is different. Each with its own smell and texture. All have character which has developed, in some cases, over centuries.'

As if on cue, we round a corner and find ourselves in front of The Grapes, a tavern that has stood here on the pebbled Limehouse Reach for nearly five hundred years. Concealed beyond the next bend we discover the equally venerable Prospect of Whitby, once known as the Devil's Tavern because of the lowlifes and cutthroats that drank there. These are places Turner and Whistler sat and sketched, where Dickens and Pepys drank their ale.

Nikita is such a devotee of the pub's humanising qualities that he's founded a new venture called PsyPub, a pub-based intellectual drop-in for anyone interested in psychology. It's warm, welcoming, fascinating and informal; a world away from the stuffy seminar. He did this partly as a reaction to the typical psychology conference.

'Sometimes we take ourselves and what we do a bit too seriously, consequently the discussion can get flat and monotonous. Actually, psychology couldn't be funnier.'

Also, this live, face-to-face coming together is Nikita's way of rebelling against what he sees as the deadening effects of social media.

'There's nothing social about it. I think of it as anti-social media. Our attention has been captured by our devices. This isn't by chance. There's tons of psychology in how they were designed to capture our attention, to activate reward mechanism, feed gratification and promote insecurity. We build personas as masks and then we wonder why we're not connecting. This is all distancing ourselves from each other. In Japan now there is a whole fad where lonely people can "rent a family" for a day. Also cuddling services where you can pay someone to hold you. No sex – just a sense of intimacy. We're losing our ability to connect with our fellow human beings. I think the best use of social media is to organise real world gatherings - like PsyPub.'

The peace of our river walk is suddenly interrupted by the beat of powerful blades and a military helicopter thwumps low over our heads.

'It's an Apache AH-64,' Nikita explains, suddenly the military nerd. 'Here we find it a curious, wasp-like thingy. If we were in a war zone, in a street in Fallujah, we'd be thinking very differently. Duck and cover. That's the power of context.'

This seems to have triggered a memory for Nikita. He arrived in Leeds with his family, aged eleven, knowing only two English phrases: 'I don't speak English' and 'Come on Baby, Light My Fire'. Home before that was a town in Russia entirely dedicated to designing and manufacturing weapons of mass destruction. It sounds a pretty eccentric place to grow up. 'Let's just say it was a very neuro-diverse population. If you are an exceptional mathematician, it doesn't mean you necessarily have comparable social skills. Genius comes at a price.

'They truly believed they were creating weapons so destructive they would make war obsolete and bring about world peace. Today we have this crazy technology that can destroy our civilisation in under an hour. It is so effective, the process would be quicker than watching a film on Netflix...'

The mood has darkened, but not for long. Nikita is a fan of the English approach to catastrophic thinking. 'I love your semi-sarcastic optimism. Doesn't matter how bad things get – impending disaster is made fun of rather than taken too seriously.'

We're approaching the iconic landmark that is Tower Bridge, its cantilevered arms closed today. Beyond is the Tower of London and the city. As we approach our destination, the lapping of the river gives way to the boom of rush hour street traffic on the bridge above.

'The world is not perfect, but the trajectory is positive. It's a good time to be alive. The best so far. People need to remind themselves of that a little bit more. Buried in every resentment and every complaint is a wish. I find it much more constructive when people tell each other what they wish for, rather than what they are unhappy about.'

11

A Fork in The Road

'When you come to a fork in the road, take it.'
Yogi Berra

**Wandering across a town or city involves complex
navigational choice-making. Properly used, the streetscape
can become a potent mechanism to help us evaluate our
options and make better, richer, more soul-centred
decisions.**

Daniel doesn't seem the kind of guy who would need creative
help. He's a professional artist working at probably the world's
leading animation studio. But even Californian hyper-creatives
have those nagging domestic decisions to make. Daniel's was:
should I sell my house now or wait? As anyone who's bought
or sold a home will tell you, this is usually a complex combination of domestic logic, market forces, financial expedience
and logistical pragmatism – with a healthy dollop of emotion
thrown in. Daniel had weighed up the pros and cons but

couldn't decide. So he arranged to attend a WalkShop (actually by volunteering to lead one) and asked the street to help him choose.

The event was held in and around the bustling, percussively mercantile market of San Francisco's Chinatown. Daniel was one of the first to leave on the quest and the last to arrive at the cafe we'd chosen for the sharing phase. As you might expect from a pro storyteller, he had a good tale to tell. Tuned up and switched on, he'd been asking his *sell-or-not-to-sell?* question as he wove his way through the crowds. At one point, on impulse, he stopped, looked up and saw a sign. Not speaking in the metaphorical, burning-bush-in-the-wilderness sense, but a shop sign, painted above a Chinese property agency, that read simply: Hang On Realty.

And that was the nudge Daniel needed to make his decision: don't sell – yet.

We've looked elsewhere in this book at how we read meaning in the street. What I want to do here is go further and look at how we can use this meaning to help make decisions. Particularly the tricky ones.

THE STREET HELPS US PHYSICALISE OUR CHOICE-MAKING...

'My brain says yes, Dad. But my body says no.'

I was just about to deliver my young daughter to a sleepover when she said this. The play date had seemed a good idea, but it was with a girl that Elsa didn't know well and she was evidently unsure. Also, the whole weekend would be in Italian; this was at a time when we were living there. We had encouraged Elsa to accept the invitation and she'd convinced herself it was a good idea – until that last minute when her body spoke up.

We all know that feeling. You've made a decision in your mind – or you're about to – and your body just doesn't agree. You feel hot under the collar. Sweaty palms. Your stomach turns.

During our wander together, we've seen how our intelligence resides throughout the body. And when it comes to making decisions – especially important ones – this intelligence wants to contribute.

Often the neuromuscular messages it sends us are very subtle, and sitting, fretting, in our offices with a coffee and biscuits for company, it's possible to miss, ignore or override this somatic conversation.

If I visit a kinesiologist, they can muscle-test me, amplifying what my body thinks about, for example, my dietary choices. I hold out my arm. Pick up a food I think I may be allergic to (in my case, all the cheeses I love) and whoosh, my arm goes weak. The verdict is unmissable. Dammit.

'By asking a muscle whether what we are presenting strengthens or weakens the energy flow, we can get to the truth without the mind being able to override it. The body doesn't lie and holds all the information we need to thrive, it is always working for us whether it feels like it or not.' That's how friend and well-being expert Lianne Campbell explains the wisdom hidden in our muscles.

But we don't always have a skilled energy medic on hand, and cheese is just one decision; we have many more (and more important ones) to make. Fortunately, we do have streets. Lots of them. And with the techniques we've been exploring in this book, the urban streetscape becomes a real-world, real-time decisionscape where choice-related metaphors like *standing at a crossroads, a parting of the ways, a fork in the road* become real and where you can explore different options to see how they feel.

If you want to test how a metaphorical U-turn might feel in work or private life, get up, go out into the street, think about the decision and make a U-turn. You'll sense whether it's the right thing for you to do because your embodied intelligence (not your brain) will tell you. It's all much more visceral than the experience of toying with columns of *pros* and *cons* on a notepad.

City design expert Tim Stonor confided to me a pet theory that 'the city is a form of computer, created in the manner of the human brain. What happens in the grid of streets? That business of serendipitous encounter, mixes and innovates like a generative computer.' Certainly, when life is disorientating, the topology of the city can help us clarify where we are and what kind of choices we need to make.

At Street Wisdom we've found there are many moment-of-truth choices that can be mapped directly on to street situations, including:

The Dead End – where you feel as though you are in a professional or personal cul-de-sac and are looking for a way out.

The Roundabout – (or Traffic Circle in North America), where you have a problem and there are too many solutions going round and round in your mind.

The No Turn – where the route you've chosen feels fixed and you're looking for an exit route. And its cousin...

The No Entry – where you've identified where you want to be/go, but the entry appears barred to you.

Whatever the choice you are facing, the street enables you to create a physical equivalent and then actively plot your way through it – live and in real time.

...ASK BETTER QUESTIONS

When people struggle to find the 'right question' to ask the street (and they often do) we encourage them to relax. Because very often the question you are asking at the start of a Walk-Shop changes as you progress.

One example that comes to mind was a middle-aged lady whose opening question was: 'What's the oldest building in this street?' I explained to her that Street Wisdom is an opportunity to solve personal questions, but she was adamant and off she went with her tourist-like, historical question in mind. As she walked, though, the experience revealed a more intimate question lurking behind the façade of an architectural one. 'I am ageing. What will I do when I retire?'

Other times, I'll meet people who have booked for an event and know at once they are not going to find what they are looking for on Street Wisdom, and that's because they have already found it. They have made their decision but don't yet realise it. This can be obvious (to the listeners, if not themselves) from the question they are asking. 'Should I stay in my lousy job or go on an adventure for a year? Or Is it time for me to have more fun in life?' The answer is already there, but the question needs adjusting. These participants shouldn't be asking the street IF, but HOW or WHEN.

Like a person who flips a coin and knows the answer they want before the coin lands, these seekers are not coming to Street Wisdom for clarity, but corroboration. Interacting with the world around us reveals a preference already hidden within us.

...INCREASE OUR OPTIONS

As we've seen, it can be useful to boil down a decision to essential choices, but this process can leave us feeling we have limited options to resolve it. As the Nobel-prize-winning economist Thomas Schelling once observed: 'One thing a person cannot do, no matter how rigorous their analysis or heroic their imagination, is to draw up a list of things that would never occur to them.'

I see this a lot when I am working with organisations and those that lead them. We can be quite binary creatures, especially under duress, and boardroom decisions all too often work their way towards a stark decision between *A or B*.

As Mark Buckle, executive learning development specialist, puts it:

> 'Decisions are the measure of a culture. If we are better informed and more sophisticated when we make decisions, we're much more in control of the destiny of our organisation. There are usually five or six layers contributing to a single decision. So the more data points you have and the more thorough and diverse they are, the better decision you are likely to make.'

When leaders are toiling at a mental fork in the road, I'll often take them out into the street and find a literal one. Standing at a junction and treating the terrain as a decision-making gym, we'll try a number of different options. Maybe the choice is actually a sequencing issue. It's not A *or* B but A *then* B. Maybe there's a hidden alley connecting the two streets, which allows you to link up A *and* B in a continuous journey. You achieve A *through* B, or B *through* A. Very often, when participants are experimenting they'll discover a completely unexpected route – C – which they prefer to either A or B.

In its complexity, the streetscape shows us there are more routes through the decision-making landscape than we originally thought. Street Wisdom participants often report they've had trial and error experiences while testing their thinking – retracing steps when the direction doesn't feel right, reversing out of dead-end streets, tracing new paths around obstacles.

As Buckle puts it, 'You realise there is far more going on than the immediate choice in front of you. It encourages you to look at things from different angles and to open yourself to the full potential. Practically, that often steers you to a different place than the one you'd predictably go.'

Physically navigating in this way activates the intelligence embodied within us and presents us with options that wouldn't otherwise have occurred to us.

...CHECK OUR BIASES

Our mental processing power is prodigious. The average waking brain crunches 11 million bits of information a second, of which our conscious mind only processes approximately forty bits. You can understand why the majority of this activity happens beneath our awareness and why our conscious thinking is guided by patterns of thought that have become usefully automated. These shortcuts are very useful because they mean we don't have to keep relearning that the green crunchy thing is called an apple or to keep discovering, painfully, that the bright flickery stuff burns. But formulaic thinking can also be a real disadvantage, especially when it comes to decision-making.

Habitual mental routines create what psychologists call cognitive bias; they guide the choices we make, whether we are aware of them or not – and very often we are not. A physical decision-making mission on the street can do the same thing, clearly mirroring back to us our hidden prejudices; once we see them, we have the option to change them.

Here are the sort of comments we often hear and the decision-making biases they uncover:

'*Normally I'd go for the first answer that comes to mind but this time I didn't.*' This participant has become aware of what is known in behavioural circles as *anchoring bias*; that is, the unconscious tendency when making a decision to focus or *anchor* on the first piece of information one hears.

'*I got an answer that seemed stupid, but instead of throwing it away as I would do at work, I kept reflecting on it and eventually it started making sense.*' Here the experience has highlighted the participant's *confirmation bias,* the tendency we have to make decisions that support our existing beliefs.

'*I normally walk at the side of the road but this time I chose to march down the middle of the pavement…*' Here's someone simply becoming aware of their inbuilt tendency to agree with what others say and do, their *conformity bias.*

'*I'd normally avoid people like that on the street…*' say people who've just met a stranger and overcome a *social/racial/stereotyping bias* of which they were not aware. There's a partner comment we also sometimes hear, along the lines of '*I am a very open/unprejudiced person…*', which reveals (to the listener, if not always the speaker) that here is a human whose unconscious bias is that they have no unconscious bias.

'*It's something I had been avoiding and when I turned a corner, there it was, staring me in the face…*' A great example of a bias known as the *ostrich effect* – the tendency to avoid or ignore decisions that may have negative implications.

Street Wisdom is deliberately designed as an extraordinary experience in an ordinary setting. It breaks the routine, so we become aware of the routine. Knowing more about the hidden biases that guide our decisions can help us make better, more conscious ones.

...RESOLVE DILEMMAS

There are times when a participant discovers that the choice they are labouring to make is not actually a choice. Sara Hope, co-founder of The Conversation Space, has a great example of this. Sara loves business. She's high-powered, high performing and totally at home in the City. She is also passionate about her home in Devon, where she lives and enjoys an uncluttered rural life. When Sara appeared at one of our events, she felt it was time to choose. Here she describes what happened on the WalkShop she attended near Liverpool Street Station on the edge of London's financial district.

'I headed first for the station. I kept repeating the question in my mind, "business or Devon", but didn't find anything significant. I was a little frustrated and frankly a bit tired. I was looking for a place to sit down when suddenly there was a break in the clouds and a shaft of sunlight illuminated an old church. There, in front, were some stone seats and one was empty. It was so dramatic I thought, *this is it!* But I was on my way over there when someone else sat in the only spare space. So that wasn't it!

'I kept thinking, kept asking and kept wandering. Eventually I came to a small square patch of grass with a tree in the middle, sculptures and a fountain. I found a park bench and flopped down. It was so quiet, it was hard to imagine we were in the City. But as I looked, I noticed how all this greenery was surrounded by skyscrapers. I just looked up at them and thought how much I loved business. At the same time I also really enjoyed the peacefulness of this quiet park. I stayed there a long while, didn't do much wandering and when it was time to leave, I looked around to find the name of this oasis. It was called... 'Sara is clearly moved remembering this '...Devonshire Square. The message for me was I don't need to choose between the city and the countryside. I can, I must, I will have both.'

Sara hadn't solved the problem in the traditional sense. Solving is, as Jung says, the province of the *ego*. Dilemmas, he says, are the purview of the *self*. That's the function of these big paradoxes we sometimes face in life. To make a good choice, Jung urges us to go inside ourselves, sit in the tension of opposites and ask: 'What is the natural urge of life, at this moment, for me?' The street, as Sara discovered, is a productive place to do this. Jung would probably have said it wasn't the street speaking to Sara in Street Wisdom, but her Self. It was up to her to figure out how she was going to reconcile the tensions of the apparent opposites (country or city?) but she emerged from Street Wisdom knowing that was what she intended to do.

Stop Press: Since her WalkShop, Sara has set up a regional office for her business in Exeter, where she can combine commercial and rural, and she continues to visit London on a regular basis. She's feeding her appetite for both the bright lights of the city and the calm of the country, all thanks to a few moments of inspired wandering.

STREET STRATEGY

The street doesn't just assist with individual decision-making.

Street Wisdom is turning out to be a potent tool for teams and organisations who are pondering what's next and don't want to base important decisions solely on whiteboard scribbles and a pile of post-it notes.

So it's appropriate that when Street Wisdom wants to think about its own future, we use a WalkShop to help us. To end this chapter, I want to share three short examples of where the navigation of our social business has been guided by our own choice-guiding, decision-enhancing system.

Straat Wisdom

I grew up in a house with a father who was a dentist. And a barrister. And a committed student with degrees in history, sociology and philosophy. And a member of the judiciary. And, for the last ten years of his life, a self-taught and exuberantly enthusiastic artist. From Bernard Pearl I learned that I didn't have to choose one career, but could enjoy several. The downside of this polyglot approach is a certain restlessness. Throughout my life I have continually been looking to the horizon and asking: 'Where next?'

A year after we first launched Street Wisdom I was feeling itchy, looking for the next thing, and David Micklem, our chairman, suggested I run my own personal WalkShop to help me figure out the next move. Fast-forward a few weeks and there I was, on Amsterdam's cobbled Westerstraat, walking in circles – again. Not leisurely big circles, but rotating around and around in a tiny area, as though trapped in an invisible tube of energy. It must have looked odd, but I didn't feel I had any alternative. I had asked the street 'where next' and within minutes I found myself pulled to this spot, like a dowsing rod twanging over an underground spring. As I rotated, the meaning became unavoidably clear to me. I had been thinking about where to go next and the street was answering me – in a way that someone as flighty as me could not avoid – '*stop here and dig*'. The immediate future wasn't about finding a project to follow Street Wisdom. Street Wisdom was the project. My job was to persist, put down roots and nurture this venture.

A Christmas Stale

A few years later, in 2016, Street Wisdom had grown and we were again looking to the future. More and more countries were trying out the experience. Where should we focus our limited energy for the greatest effect? As the year came towards its end, we were all suffering from a bit of fatigue. We were jaded. My own mood was not helped by the fact that I was in a gloomy New York that seemed in shock from Trump's divisive election win and the city was self-medicating with a grosser than normal pre-Xmas consumer binge.

With some important strategic decisions only days away, I had put some time aside for a solo WalkShop. I confess my personal question was: 'Is this all worth it?' What difference could our little social venture make in a world that seemed to me to be heading the wrong way fast? I went into the tune-up with low energy so I wasn't prepared for the shock I was about to get. Pearl, Pearl, Pearl, Pearl, Pearl… I was passing a newsstand and New York was blaring my name. I didn't realise at the time that it was the seventy-fifth anniversary of the attack on Pearl Harbour and furled magazines (with the word Harbour tucked over) were referring to history, not to me. But it woke me up and initiated one of the most informative WalkShops I've experienced.

At its heart was a conversation I had with Daniel, a barista in a funky new Samsung store filled with virtual reality games and experiences. He was one of those inspiring strangers you seem to meet on Street Wisdom just when you need to. Enjoying a hand-made coffee amid all the VR, I told him a little about our street venture and asked him his advice. What, for him, a hipster in the digital age, would be the point of Street Wisdom in a world where people seem to be mesmerised by technology but sealed off from the wonders happening around them. Daniel explained how much people need a dose of genuine reality to balance all the virtual reality now available. Also, as someone who was synchronistically enough involved in the non-profit movement, he reminded me it's important to get the funding handled elegantly if you want to do good without getting worn down.

It reinforced my confidence in Street Wisdom and made me realise the value of the methodology not only to the public but also to business. We put new focus on creating work with businesses interested in exploring the power of experience for their staff and customers. Oh, and our first major client a couple of months later? It was a company who wanted to transform their UK outlets from traditional shops to experiential stores, a company called Samsung.

Choices, Choices

The third short story I want to share happened almost exactly a year later. Same month, different continent, and very different weather.

In case you didn't know (and I had definitely forgotten) December in Sydney can be sizzling hot. Wandering through the Surry Hills district felt a bit like sauntering through a kiln. But I was emerging from an intense period of work and felt I needed to come up for air – even if that air felt like a blast from a blowtorch.

Uncoupled from the day-to-day, I started to think about the

rest of my life: what I wanted to do with it and the part Street Wisdom might play.

It might have been my philosophical mood or mild heat-stroke, but the street didn't mince its words. The text came fully formed into my mind, like a message in a bottle from the future. Here, word for word, are the notes I made immediately after.

> Imagine a complete range of futures – from the awful to wonderful – is possible for us and our planet. And that what determines where we end up is the quality of the choices we make – individually and collectively – from now onwards. If you care about the future, help yourself and your fellow humans make choices our future deserves. That's the mission.

Helping humans make better choices. Those few words have stayed with me as a deeper 'why' running through all my work – particularly Street Wisdom. I mention them here in the hope that you will find it a compelling context to let Street Wisdom assist you in your own decision-making.

When you, I or any of us make decisions that are smart and heartfelt, intuitive, conscious and soul driven, everyone benefits. Let's collectively make those choices our future deserves. New navigation for new times.

EXERCISE: HUMAN COMPASS

What?

This exercise, inspired by the work of Arnold Mindell, gives a direct experience of our embodied, inner guidance system and how it can guide us towards what we need to learn.

Why?

Making decisions, particularly demanding ones, can leave us 'going round and round in our heads': lots of circular mental motion, but very little physical action or resolution. This exercise is a way of moving the decision-making process out of our minds and into our bodies. Rather than thinking about the best path to take, we let our body decide for us and follow where it leads.

How?

Find a space in a street outside. Ideally an open space (plaza or square) where you have room to wander safely. Take a moment to 'tune up' (see chapter 4). A simple way is to close your eyes, breathe slowly and connect with whatever you are feeling inside.

Now think of a decision you want to make and imagine the 'right' choice is waiting for you somewhere out in the street. Let your body turn on the spot until it senses it is pointing towards where the answer awaits.

Open your eyes and follow that direction for fifty steps. Work round any major obstacles if you have to. When the fifty steps are done, stop and take a good look (and listen and smell) around. How does what you are experiencing help with the decision? If you really connect with what's happening, there's pretty much always something helpful to learn.

If that's not conclusive – or even if it is – close your eyes again, let your body find a new bearing and walk, for forty paces this time. And continue, reducing the number of steps by ten every time.

If the answer is inconclusive, try reframing the decision in a way that forces you to make a clear choice. Or maybe accept this is a decision you just don't want to make right now.

You can see a digital version of this exercise here: streetwisdom.org/wanderful-exercises/

'I am going to take you somewhere interesting.' I'd been looking forward to seeing the city through Bruce's eyes, but hadn't quite anticipated his upbeat pace. As we barrel along Air Street and across Piccadilly, it occurs to me that velocity is a word that suits him well.

I am interrupting a senior executive of a major company in the middle of the afternoon, but he seems keen to get out and about.

Bruce is flying along but taking it all in. Almost without breaking his step, he bends down to pick up a plastic bottle that someone has carelessly discarded on the pavement and pops it into a recycling bin. There's no bravado or speech about ridding the environment of plastic. 'One a day,' he says simply. 'I just do one a day...' And we've moved on.

'I love this square.'

We've arrived at a picture-perfect little park encased in railings and surrounded by imposing eighteenth-century London architecture.

'London has these beautiful oases – like little parks filled with all these mature trees where you can escape. A few years back I was witnessing burnout in the people around me. The fact I was diagnosing it in others means I was probably feeling it a bit myself. So I became fascinated in the science of lunch breaks. I just started coming down here with a book, to try to force myself not to be sitting on my phone. And I discovered it's just so good for your energy – your sanity.

'There's a lot of talk about the why of work, its purpose. For me it's more about learning more of the how of work – how can I feel happier day-to-day?'

Bruce's curiosity about how to make work better spawned the UK's most popular business podcast (Eat Sleep Work Repeat) as well as a No. 1 bestselling book, *The Joy of Work*. He's managed both, alongside his not inconsiderable day job, running Twitter's business in Europe, the Middle East and Asia.

Like I said – velocity. But I am finding Bruce somehow does swiftness in a way that doesn't feel speedy or stressful. Not for one moment while I am with him do I sense he wants to be somewhere else.

'I love this part of town. We are so used to London being this sprawling metropolis it's easy to forget it used to be so rural. There's an amazing pub over the road called the Blue Posts, referring to the way they used to mark out the hunting grounds. Imagine how different London looked then, political classes down here and people hunting up there.'

While he likes the rural, Birmingham-born Bruce derives energy from cities.

'I love the energy of cities. Can't imagine not living in one. I was just speaking to an organisation [note: don't tell anyone but it was the intelligence service MI5] and they asked me, "Where would you most like to wake up in the world?"

'I just thought, what an honour to wake up in this city. I love London.'

We've darted across Pall Mall. Well, Bruce darted, I tried to keep up, and now we're weaving through St James's Park. The greenery's lush. The air is chilly but the sky is clear, and all feels abundant. This sets Bruce's mind off in a new direction.

'The only thing I'd say is that a wonderful, functioning city has to be affordable and that's a challenge right now. I struggle to see how someone who's barely bringing in a few pounds is going to be able to live in this city. There are parts of this town that used to be dedicated to specific things like music and the arts. It's tragic. If you haven't got artists doing counterculture, the culture dies a bit, doesn't it? I hope we don't lose something magical about this place.'

Bruce stops in his tracks and locks eyes with a pelican standing watching us beadily from the side of the lake. 'Love that pelican. Look at him. His neck's in and he's cold. It's like he's saying, you promised me summer...'

Bruce is chuckling, and that, turns out to be right at the heart of why he's so interested in improving the workplace.

'I love laughing. I was obsessed with sitcoms as a kid. It's a good day at work for me when I've laughed till it hurt at least three times. Some of the places I have worked in have been laughter filled. Others – hmm – less so. That's partly why I am so interested in avoiding that dead-eyed burnout and getting a bit more mojo back into work.

'So many people don't find their workplaces are clicking and functioning in the way they want. I was wondering why and became completely bewitched with the idea of human synchronisation. It's something I first came across in this lecture by Brian Eno,[1] where he talks about how art allows us to synchronise with each other.

'There's so much evidence that humans desire to connect in this way with other humans. I'm thinking about the famous experiment where the psychologist and anthropologist Robin Dunbar put two groups of rowers on rowing machines. He told one group to row each at their own speed and the others to find a shared rhythm. When he tested their endorphin levels afterwards, the group that had been in sync could take twice the level of pain as the group that hadn't.

'When we feel synchronised with other humans beings, there's this magical energy created. Just ask people who march or dance or sing together. That's why people who aim to build movements often appropriate those collective activities. But synchronisation is a real challenge with modern work. Over the last fifteen years we've devolved away from a lot of things that synchronise us – like face-to-face chatting. Workplaces have become disconnected and less empathetic.'

1 https://bbc.in/2N18ztn

As a prominent leader in a global company, how has Bruce sought to counteract that tendency?

'In work, I never want to take the sense of agency away from people. Most of modern work infantilises us. That's why I am obsessive about having fewer meetings with fewer participants. When you look at psychological safety, candour, transparent dialogue, they are all difficult to accomplish when meetings are big. If you're with two colleagues you're far more likely to say why their idea won't work than if you're with thirty colleagues. In big meetings, the mindset is "if the boss wants his folly, let him have it". Smaller teams remove the burden of keeping everyone in the loop.

'So I'm ruthless about keeping things smaller and more agile. Dunbar pointed out that people can only trust a maximum of about 150 people. It's about the capacity of your cerebral neocortex. Sure we can have relationships with more than 150 but we won't have the same visceral trust. The problem is, even with 150 people, 45 per cent of your time is taken up with maintaining those relationships, and you see that in modern organisations all the time.

'Conventional wisdom says it's more efficient to centralise functions like marketing and HR, but if you do that, things quickly stop being meaningful. People feel they are just implementing someone else's orders.'

While conventional wisdom isn't his thing, Bruce is clearly a wisdom seeker. Every week in his podcast he is turning over stones looking for new insights and fresh ideas, and he's open about where that wisdom comes from.

While his is a relatively youthful company, he thinks 'there's a danger in fetishising the young. Mark Zuckerberg is supposed to have claimed that young people are innately smarter than older ones. I think that's more an insight into how the young and entitled see the world. At the same time, I don't hold with the heuristic that says older equals wiser. Looking at how the vested interests operate, I am worried we still have a system that believes people of a certain age have a wisdom that is bestowed upon them. That's self-evidently not true.'

We're nipping along Haymarket now and Bruce shares a clue to his impressive drive.

'What really energises me is the fact that two of my closest friends today are people I didn't know half a year ago. I love the sense of renewal and discovery you get when you meet new people who surprise you and challenge what you think.

'I have got to know this poet, Hussain Manawer, very well. I saw him at an event and he really moved me. I chatted to him and asked if there was anything I could do to help him. We hung out a bit in the park and became very good mates. It's funny but he'd never sat in a park before. He told me he'd seen people doing that but hadn't realised why. It's great to be reminded that what's special to you isn't necessarily special to everyone.'

We've found ourselves back outside his offices and just before he bounds back inside, Bruce bends down, picks up a plastic bottle and pops it in a recycling bin.

'Just one a day,' he repeats. But I think he's talking about a Bruce Daisley day.

Like I said – velocity.

...

12

Connection Cafe

> *'No man is an island'*
> *John Donne, Meditation 17, Devotions on Emergent Occasions*

**Street Wisdom culminates with participants gathering to
share their experiences and collectively consider what they
have learned. Here we reflect on some of the lessons of
Wanderful, as well as navigational clues about the way
forward.**

In the final phase of a Street Wisdom WalkShop, the participants who've each been wandering the streets on their solo
'quests' find their way back together – usually at a cafe, bar or
pub. Here, while enjoying tea, coffee or something stronger,
they share their experiences with each other (provided they
want to, that is; there is no pressure). I named this session, with
some considerable lack of imagination, The Sharing, and it's
come to be a far more important part of the process than originally expected.

Around the cafe table we ask members of the group (and, remarkably, these groups of strangers who only met an hour or two before now, do feel like a real group) to consider two questions: *What happened?* and *What (if anything) did you learn?* We added the 'if anything' to remove pressure from anyone who didn't feel the experience was particularly instructive and/or who are going to need more than an hour to really internalise what they've learned.

The Sharing was intended to function as a kind of airlock where participants could adjust from what are often quite intense street experiences and prepare for their return to so-called reality – the name we give to the overlooked miracle of 'normal' life.

I expected this session to be useful, but hadn't anticipated how much people would enjoy it, often choosing to overrun the sixty minutes we allocated for it in the WalkShop process.

Participants swap notes (and contact details) and compare their experiences. People discover how different their experiences have been, but also how similar. They think about 'where next, what then?', and linking their experience back to their original question, it's the moment the penny drops for many.

As we approach the end of our own shared stroll through *Wanderful*, I thought you and I could do something similar. Let's find a cafe table, get something to drink (mine's a double espresso – sorry, a hopeless caffeine addict) and take a moment to reflect.

Wanderful has been a bit of a personal quest for me: nearly a year to write and, before that, nearly a decade of exploration, which is why I'd like to step out of the authorial role now, join you at the table and ask myself the questions we ask Street Wisdom participants.

What happened? We've covered quite a bit of ground in our literary saunter. We've looked at the origins of the Street Wisdom approach, tuned up our embodied intelligence and pressed the syn-chronicity button. Then we wandered through a rabbit warren of connected ideas, kinking our straight-line thinking, decoding signs, adjusting our walking (and life) tempo, intentionally straying to see what we'd find, encountering wise as well as scary strangers and finally making some new choices about making new choices.

And *what (if anything) did I learn?* Running Street Wisdom and now writing about it, I've learned a lot. With your permission, I am going to note down a few lessons that really stand out. That's partly so I don't forget. As we say in The Sharing, *what you say now, you get to remember.* But also so I can use these realisations to help navigate a way forward – both for myself and for the social venture.

While these are personal conclusions and very much addressed to myself, I hope some of what the street told me speaks to you too.

GENEROSITY DOES WORK

Street Wisdom is valuable and there have been many moments where I and my colleagues have questioned 'giving it away' to the public. But the atmosphere of generosity this has generated around the project is more than worth it. Instead of protecting and policing the work, we've made it super accessible so it can spread quickly round the world. Rather than getting caught up defending our-selves from property theft, we figured it's very hard to steal some-thing that's being offered as a gift. And like appears to attract like. Street Wisdom's open-handed approach has magnetised open-hearted, generous souls and organisations towards it. Many of those organisations have engaged Street Wisdom in commercial work and that revenue now helps to fund our mission. So generosity pays, too. While the compact we have with users is not financial, we do make requests (use with integrity, follow the instructions carefully, send us your stories and so on…) and people have honoured the spirit of the exchange. So, David, when you come to future forks in the business road, just keep in mind that generosity works.

SYNCHRONISE, YOU IDIOT

The idiot is me, not you. Seeing how amazingly synchronicity supports you, it's idiotic not to rely on it every moment – and still I forget. You can spend your life trying to make stuff happen or seeing what wants to happen and helping it. The latter is much easier and more graceful. Something to remember: if you see me forgetting that, friend, please nudge me.

THE NEW WORKPLACE

I originally took clients out of their offices into the streets as an alternative to the workplace. I realise now the streets are actually a new workplace. More vibrant, physical, stimulating than an office building and free to use.

YOUR CREATIVE PLAYMATE

Great ideas don't come from you or me but from the space between us. That's why creatives often work in pairs, throwing ideas back and forth. But a lot of us don't have that luxury. We are expected (and expect ourselves) to navigate creative challenges solo. When you think of the street as an entity, not a location, things get interesting. Suddenly the world outside becomes your creative partner. The more you play with it, the more playful it will be in return.

THANK YOU, TREES

Spending a lot of time on streets, you really notice the trees. Normally they are shoved to the side of our consciousness, a town planner's afterthought, plonked there to pimp up our civic spaces. But they're wonderful. They work patiently to transform our belching, petrochemical by-product into breathable air. They provide shade and visual calm. Connecting with trees, even just looking at one, can be an express lift to more meditative states. That's why I always encourage volunteer leaders to start their Street Wisdom Walk-Shops close to, and ideally under, the energetic canopy of a tree. So, trees – large or small and yes, bushes, you too – in case I forget to do this to you individually, I am sending you a group hug. Thanks. And, sitting here, right now, a penny just dropped. As a sign of my gratitude, I plan to plant more of you. A lot more.

DON'T THINK, MOVE

People are always saying to me 'we need to sit down and sort this out'. We don't. Because if we do, we won't. Sitting is not thinking. Witness the endless political deadlocks that are daily enacted by immobile folks staring at each other across a table. We are three-dimensional. To think, we need to move. 'My mind works only with my legs.' The philosopher Rousseau said it. I just didn't listen until recently.

THERE IS NO 'OUT THERE' OUT THERE

My own personal WalkShops, and the hundreds I have led for others, have shown me that the experience you are having of the street is actually an experience of yourself. You are walking through you. That's why everyone's time on the same streets is so completely different. But, there's a twist. Stay with the experience and the personal expands to become much more universal. Little 'me' becomes a big and encompassing 'we'. Hard to describe but enlightening to experience. So, keep practising, David.

WONDER IS A DECISION

If you're looking to experience wonder, nowhere is better than anywhere else. You don't have to wait for the wonders to come along. You choose to see them. Sure, there are some backdrops that might help us more easily work our wonder muscle, but I have stood in some pretty amazing places in the world and seen people look as bored and fretful as they might in a traffic jam on their own city street. There's a reason the secondary meaning of wonder is to 'desire to know something'. Curiosity is the trigger. If you want to discover wonder, and live a more 'wanderful' life, then just when others are settling for reality, get intrigued, get inquisitive: go for a wander.

OCCUPY THE STREETS

When the public wants to make its feelings known, it traditionally 'takes to the streets'. Revolutions often begin – and many regimes have ended – there. I am sure we will see more of this. But while streets are increasingly associated with out-pourings of anger and frustration, it doesn't need to be that way. Street Wisdom has shown me that we should occupy the streets (after all, they are ours) for more creative ends, to spark a revolution of curiosity, perhaps, or to ignite a mass movement of friendliness or overturn the urban status quo and make our cities more lovable and loving.

ROUGH (IN)JUSTICE

The number of people living on the streets or 'sleeping rough', as we euphemistically say, is increasing. You can't fail to be aware of this on our WalkShops. On one recent event in San Francisco (epi-centre of tech wealth), we were picking our way through a for-est of cardboard and sleeping bags. Evidence of a broken system or a result of California's warm climate… Homelessness is on the increase worldwide. I know my response (the occasional interac-tion here, donation there) is wholly inadequate. I am not sure what I and/or Street Wisdom can do to help. Still, I hold on to an experi-ence I had many years ago when, struggling with my own mental stability, I found myself virtually 'on the streets'. Sitting on a bench one afternoon, lost in my anxieties, I noticed a group of rough sleepers approaching. Acting on impulse, I reached into my pocket for some loose change, but they didn't want money. They wanted to help. Did I have somewhere to stay? If not, they could make space for me. It was a low point, sure. But a turning point too, as I realised '*they* are me'. The homeless people we pass on the streets are *us* – minus a bit of luck. I try to remember and act accordingly and often fail. So this isn't a lesson learned, but a pledge to keep learning.

David Pearl

FOLLOW THE LEADER?

As manoeuvring your way down a swirling city street reminds us, this is a complex, perplexing world and most of us are blundering our way through it. People who seem to offer a clear direction stand out. But be careful, there's no one way forward. Uncertain times throw up ambitious people with clear, often self-serving ideas about the way ahead. To me they look a bit like those slightly desperate types standing in a crowd of passing pedestrians with a fluorescent 'Unbelievable Deals This Way' sign. But they only become leaders if we follow them. From what I have seen and learned in the last few years, the only leaders I am going to be following in future are ones that have a clear intention, a *why* that I can relate to, but don't pretend theirs is the only route. As my colleague Rasmus Hougaard, founder and MD of the Potential Project, puts it, rebooting the words of the Buddha: "There is no path for leadership in the new era. Leading is the path". Rather than follow a confident huckster off a cliff, I'd rather fall in behind decently doubting humans who are prepared to sense the way forward – folk who learn as they go, reverse out of cul-de-sacs when necessary, consult heart, gut and body as much as head. Above all, let's favour leadership that's itself led by wisdom, not by ideology, unfounded self-belief and/or by mining databases full of our information. And remember, David, if you come across someone in the street offering an unbelievable deal, it's probably just that.

SO WHAT'S NEXT?

Throughout *Wanderful*, alongside my personal questions I have also been asking what's next for Street Wisdom. Our mission is to bring inspiration to every street on Earth so, while we have made great strides so far, there's a long, long way to go.

The experience of preparing, researching and writing *Wanderful* has thrown up many navigational clues about how our social venture might make even more impact. In addition to our existing public and business activities, here are three future directions the street is, I think, nudging us to explore further.

Experience learning

An explosion of digital learning, plus the growing cost and frustration with conventional education methods, has unleashed a huge appetite for 'experiential learning': learning by doing. Learners like to get their information online but their teaching live. Experience is how the younger us learned our way around the world. We internalise what we experience quicker than what we read and tend to remember it longer. Experiential learning is a new term for an age-old idea. Picture the peripatetic Aristotle teaching as he wandered about the agora with his students. But I see huge potential right now for this approach, especially in the streets, which are an inexhaustible source of stimulus and – free. Think of how we use street-related words like *way, path* and *course* metaphorically to describe the *learning journey*. Street Wisdom is a chance to experience that journey in a real, visceral way. This is particularly appealing to the experience-hungry younger generation that are growing into adulthood now. Not only can a methodology like this bring a refreshing new dimension to traditional educational subjects but, we're finding it's useful for students thinking in a more macro-way about their futures. This is a difficult world to choose career paths in. And many young people feel the pressure is really on them to make what feel like life-shaping decisions. There isn't a Street Wisdom specifically for young people – not yet. But we're already talking to teachers and career counsellors about how to help our future citizens find their way through the maze and make the sort of intuitively intelligent choices they can trust.

Sacred cities

This is going to be an urban century. A sustainable future means we *have* to live in cities. So let's make them places we *want* to live.

One of the impulses behind Street Wisdom was to explore the wonders that are right on our doorsteps. I'm not a conventionally religious person but I do find myself thinking about the lure of pilgrimages and the ritualistic power of walking, intentionally, to a spiritually important destination. What's our modern equivalent of that? Why can't we bring a bit of that sacredness to the average high street? Or rather, find it? Because it's already there.

Wisdom streets

Street Wisdom events come and go. But do they have to? In a project we're calling Wisdom Streets, we've begun exploring with local councils how to create areas where the spirit of Street Wisdom is hardwired into a town. Early experiments show it could be a powerful way to kick-start regeneration, revitalise high streets and, most importantly, stimulate community.

I'm not in the prediction business but all the contemporary divination I've done with Street Wisdom and elsewhere convinces me that we don't make it to the future alone. Individualism is too isolating and wasteful. The way forward is to think, work and live more communally.

Just step back and take a look at our little cafe gathering. It's not just you and I any more. The place has filled with people finishing their WalkShops around the world. Not only them, but all the characters we've met so far in the book, including our illustrious strangers. Ken, Charles, Suzy, Pati... all of you, come and grab a seat.

When we step back together and view the scene, we see what community looks like, particularly the energy that's available when people gather with a simple shared intent. It sounds like a cliché, but it's true. No man or woman is an island. Inspired by that idea, I want to invite you on one final wander together.

INVOLVED IN HUMANKIND

Picture us stepping out into the street in London. It's evening and we're near St Paul's Cathedral. The first thing you notice is that it doesn't have Christopher Wren's majestic dome. That is nearly fifty years away from being built. This is London in the year 1623 and the old St Paul's we are looking at was built in the Gothic style, with a towering spire and a wooden roof. That's one of the reasons it is doomed to burn so fiercely when the Great Fire of London comes.

Let's step round to the Cathedral close, where the clergy live, and imagine a lighted window in an upstairs room. There we find a man writing. John Donne is Dean of St Paul's, but will be known to future generations as one of the greatest metaphysical poets. He's recovering from a near fatal illness – probably typhus – and this evening he is meditating on his brush with death. Looking over his shoulder, we can see those five immortal words: *No man is an island.* He's just finishing the piece; it's more a meditation than a poem, with the equally famous line: *for whom the bell tolls.* I have always thought this was some sort of grim warning about the approach of death, but as we read the whole text, we realise the message is different and has real meaning for us today.

> 'No man is an island entire of itself; every man is a piece of the continent, a part of the main; if a clod be washed away by the sea, Europe is the less, as well as if a promontory were, as well as any manner of thy friends or of thine own were; any man's death diminishes me, because I am involved in mankind. And therefore never send to know for whom the bell tolls; it tolls for thee.'

Being 'involved in humankind' means accepting we are all deeply, intricately and inextricably connected. We're all part of the same continent. When anyone dies, we all die a little.

These words move me greatly and inspire me. I realise now, Street Wisdom can play a part in helping us to explore our essential connectedness – to each other and the world around us, and also to recognise that our future direction is a shared one. While Street Wisdom is designed as a navigation aid for the self, it's morphing into a resource for our collective onward journey, helping us all tune in to the wisdom around and within, to feel our way across the stones and make decisions the future deserves.

Funny that we're ending the book with poetry. Just as we started. Not what I intended. But there it is. Synchronicity.

And then I hear a bell tolling – for me. Actually, it's my iPhone reminding us that time's up. Back in the connection cafe, there's no sign of things tailing off. People are 'involved in mankind' – doing it, not talking about it. It looks like a party, but it feels like a movement. And who knows where it can lead us?

Wanderful

Charles is the sort of stranger you'll naturally find yourself talking to. Something about him invites you to stop him and ask a question. But if you do, he's more than likely to ask you one back. As organisations around the world have discovered when they've turned to him for a bit of wisdom, he's reluctant to hand out answers.

'It seems to me so much in this world has gone wrong that when people come and tell me they have the answer, I immediately doubt they are right. And so I ask questions and look for alternatives. All my life has been about questioning people's opinions.'

As we pad through parkland, Charles explains that this appetite for questioning which he calls 'decent doubt', started when he was growing up, a clergyman's son in rural Ireland.

'I kept pretty quiet but seriously started doubting as a teenager, starting with stories of the New Testament. It seemed to me that they often took everyday occurrences and gave them huge religious significance. I didn't ever tell my father as I thought it would hurt him, being so disrespectful. Although I later suspected he probably thought much the same.

'Later on I had this funny job at Windsor Castle [yes, I'm sure you've got questions about Charles's unconventional career, but let's keep strolling and we'll come back to that...], effectively, educating future bishops about life. They were parish priests concerned with family life who suddenly found themselves having to be civic figures. They knew next to nothing about business or trade unions or politics, and so we tried to help. In the process, I discovered most don't really believe what they say they believe. Their role had become a bit like a hymn we sing without thinking about the words. Trapped in a routine.'

As his career path testifies, Charles is no routine-lover: oil executive turned teacher turned business school pioneer turned author turned social philosopher, with some bishop-wrangling and equipment lugging [for his photographer wife, Elizabeth] thrown in for good measure. That said, the younger Charles was very nearly caught in the 'fur-lined rut' of a predictable corporate life.

'I grew up in the middle of Ireland and was educated in a boarding school and then Oxford, so I felt very cloistered and wanted to get out. I didn't really know where and Shell decided that for me. I remember we were on a management training course and at the end, our mentor brought in fourteen envelopes, one for each of the participants. Inside was our destiny. Mine said "Kuala Lumpur", a place I had never heard of, but I went along. It took me a long time to question that part of my life. I was timid, in a sense.'

Enter the redoubtable Elizabeth, Charles's wife of 55 years. Sidebar: Liz was also my photography teacher. The pictures in this book are dedicated to her memory.

'My wife had no respect for organisations or rules or anything like that. When she heard I was being posted to Africa to lead the business in Liberia, she was outraged. "You're not going to go, are you?" I explained it was a big compliment to be asked to run a whole country for the company. She didn't buy it. "I didn't realise I was marrying a man who would go where he was told by people he didn't even know and apparently aspired to being one of those people – and then do the same to others. Did you know you were that sort of man?"'

'Did you know you were that sort of man?' Ouch. So Charles was not the only Great Questioner in the household.

'Yes, Liz created a healthy doubt for me. She questioned all rules and regulations. Was X really sensible? Why is Y necessary? Do you really want to do Z? Shell was a very safe place. I thought I'd bumble around the world getting ever bigger houses until I retired at sixty-two and die eighteen months later, as their data predicted I would. I was a puppet really. She was quite right to haul me out of it.'

There are routines Charles does love, and this morning walk is one of them. He takes the same route at the same time every day so that he doesn't have to think about directions and can clear his mind. He calls it his walking meditation. We're strolling amiably along. Easy pace. Skirting the pub where we are going to have lunch later. The big city is just on the other side of the dual carriageway, but it seems a world away.

Charles has thought and written a lot about the power of reinventing yourself through your life. He paints a picture of life as a series of curves, the art being to catch your next curve before the one you are on peters out of energy. Hang on too long to what's safe and familiar and you can expect to find yourself at what Charles picturesquely calls 'Davey's Bar'. A vestigial, Irish lilt comes into his voice as he says the name, conjuring a darkened hostelry where quietly embittered souls mutter away their afternoons talking of what might have been.

A curve or two after Shell, Charles found himself in the world of academia and tempted again into certainty.

'When I started lecturing at business school, I did start suggesting all kinds of solutions. But I quickly realised that was rather silly because I don't really know any answers. Also, the businesses I'd use as exemplars would inevitably make huge mistakes. I found it much more interesting to get people to work it out for themselves – with a little help and prodding along the way.

'Challenging people to work things out for themselves – I think basically that's what learning's all about.'

Charles isn't one for labels, but if you push him he'll admit to being 'a bit of an amateur philosopher'.

'My theory is that philosophers give you answers that are actually questions. For example, I like to paraphrase Aristotle's Eudaimonia as "doing the best at what you're best at for the good of everyone". It sounds very simple until you ask yourself "what am I best at?" and "am I doing the best with it?" and "is it for other people or myself?". Actually, Aristotle is posing three questions in one statement.

'Again, I often say "everyone has a golden seed in them that, if they can discover it, will really give a point to their life". It's a statement, but actually it's a question because you are left wondering, "what is my golden seed?"'

I have personal proof that Charles's method works. Over the years he's asked me several life-altering questions that have stuck there, gently tickling my mind, gradually nudging me towards an answer. Years ago, he asked mildly: 'Do you really need all those people in your organisation?' Today my organisation is me. Plus a network of really capable, wonderfully creative independent people who work together when necessary to get work done.

Today, though world renowned, Charles is also a one-man band – literally so, since his wife died in 2018. But walking has one rule (along with Take No Taxis!) that he and Liz, his norm-challenging soulmate, did follow. 'You don't know a city until you walk it,' he says. And this daily walk through the park is part of his working process. 'It helps me empty my mind so I can get down to things. I ponder. I plan my day. Exactly what am I going to do and write? What's my purpose?'

Lunch beckons. So what questions is the Questioner-in-Chief asking himself as we meander along towards lunch and a glass of Guinness?

'I am thinking about the idea of "Life after life". What do you do when you've done all you meant to do? It was an idea that arose when Liz and I were sitting in a vineyard in South Africa a month before she died. We were thinking about what we were going to do next and reckoned we had done everything we wanted to do.' Charles says this with a smile and some satisfaction. 'We could think of projects, of course, but not ones we really wanted to commit to. She'd just bought a wonderful new camera but didn't really know what she wanted to shoot with it. We're not the sort of people who want to go on cruises or play golf. We've always had a purpose-driven life in a way. So it's a real question. What does life after life mean and how do you live it?'

And he adds, almost as an afterthought: 'And wouldn't it be nice if we could die when we wanted to?'

These are serious questions and they hang in the air along with the birdsong.

But lest we start taking ourselves too seriously, Charles gives the last word to his ten-year-old grandson. A chip off the old block, Sam has begun studying philosophy at junior school. Intrigued, Charles asked him to define philosophy. 'Philosophy is...' – Sam paused for the right words, '...one big question and lots of answers.'

Quite! Time for that beer.

13

Next Steps

'Next steps…' is a term that strikes fear into the hearts of any-one who has ever sat through a business meeting. It usually means this is where all the work gets parcelled out and you get landed a long list of to-dos.

Relax. The next steps I am thinking about here are literal ones, thinking about the direction you might want to wander in from here. I am totally confident you'll find your own way without my advice – especially with *Wanderful*'s navigational techniques to help you – but there are three broad directional suggestions we offer WalkShop participants when they com-plete their events, and I thought you might find them helpful nudges.

We call them *take it up, leave it be* and *pass it on.*

Take it up
The techniques I have shared in this book can be used any time, anywhere. Like I said earlier, they are like access codes to

some deeper dimensions of daily reality. Now you have them, you can log in whenever you want.

If you are coming to the end of this book with unanswered questions (and Street Wisdom participants often do), the good news is there are lots more streets out there and lots of time – if you take it – to wander them.

You can do this by yourself, but you could also, if you wanted, find a Street Wisdom WalkShop. Even lead one yourself (see below).

Remember, too, the street doesn't end in the street. Though we've been concentrating here on the phenomena you encounter *out there* in the street, you can bring all that sensitivity and insight, the playfulness and magic, into the workplace and home with you.

Leave it be

It goes without saying – so I'll say it. You can leave these ideas right where they are. If you don't feel wanderfulness is for you, or it's not (yet) time, walk away and keep browsing. There's probably something that's perfect for you round the next corner. Just pay attention.

Pass it on

If you want to share the wonder of wandering with your friends and family, you'll find event details at streetwisdom.org. If you can't see a WalkShop near you right now, you're welcome to download our Wandercast audio guide. Install it on your smartphone and let me take you through the process at a time that suits you.

As we've mentioned before, Street Wisdom events are led by volunteers around the world. One of the powerful ways to experience one of our WalkShops is to lead one. You'll find instructions about how to do that, and lots of support assets, on our site.

Many of our volunteers like to stay connected with each other and learn more. For them, we've created a Members Club with an interactive Slack platform, creative missions and online webinars. If you'd like to know more, please get in touch.

And finally, business. As the Street Wisdom movement spreads around the world, businesses, government and non-profit organisations are seeing the value of this new school of the streets for their own people. In response, we create bespoke, professionally facilitated experiential learning events tuned to an organisation's needs; that includes tasters, half-day and full-day experiences. If you think your organisation could benefit, please get in touch, and if hard-nosed colleagues think it all sounds a bit odd and un-businessy, we have case studies aplenty to share. Leading HR thinker and blogger David D'Souza (head of the CIPD in London) has called Street Wisdom 'an incredible tool and important movement, whether for personal exploration or to encourage creativity in business'.

So that's it. For now. I've really enjoyed our wander together. I hope to see you somewhere down the street, sometime. Until then, have a wanderful time.

Street Wisdom

Thousands of people have already experienced Street Wisdom's unique free WalkShops around the world.

Here's what some of them say:

'Street Wisdom was like turning the volume up on my eyes.' Liz, London, UK

'What an amazing experience! I'm still surprised by what I felt. When you allow them to, the streets really speak to you.' Andrea, Mexico City, Mexico

'The session was truly inspiring. I find it hard to slow down, but this... This opens a new, or actually existing but unseen reality to me...' Niels, Amsterdam, Netherlands

'It's hard to explain how it all works but it really helps you process the important questions we often find we can't answer.' CJ, London, UK

'There is so much abundance of stimuli and people busy fighting their way through, a lot of it goes unnoticed. But it's there.' Lucy, New York, USA

'Full of creativity, full of surprises, we've come to terms with quite a bit. I've seen so many new things and had so many new experiences. It's been amazing to be a part of it.' Antonia, Nairobi, Kenya

'There's inspiration everywhere, and Street Wisdom helps you see it in new ways, as if your very eyeballs had been replaced!' Chris, London, UK

'I was amazed how the process brought me into a different state of being, allowing me to think in different ways than ever before.' Cecily, Wellington, New Zealand

'Sometimes Street Wisdom delivers immaculate insights, sometimes it reframes the questions and refines them, articulates them. But it always benefits the participants in seeing and feeling more comprehensively.' Chris, Alicante, Spain

'It was amazing. I've been to Sheffield many times before but that day I looked at it differently. So differently it changed my life.' Phil, Sheffield, UK

'This was a confirmation that when you look for something and you sincerely want to find it, reality responds with very clear signs.' Gazzella, Damanhur, Italy

'When we slow down and go a little bit inside our bodies, we remind ourselves that we are craving more wholesome day to day experiences of life. The great thing is that we don't have to go very far to start having these experiences.' Vernon, London, UK

'A truly unique experience that brought me back in contact

with my inner self and walked me around Paris using my instincts.' Mylène, Paris, France

'I move so fast both in body and mind that I miss out on all the different and interesting things around me. Which made me think, how much in my life have I just walked right past and missed out on. 23 years of missing out on things that could have enriched my life.' Bea, London, UK

'What is insignificant becomes significant.' Katie, Leicester, UK

'I think of Street Wisdom as a live experiment, a process to reset your mind and rethink your approach to everything from creativity to problem solving.' Ian, London, UK

'Street Wisdom was an enlightening experience! The city I've called home for nearly 15 years beckoned me to go deeper and to see her in a completely new light.' Chris, San Francisco, USA

'Usually when I walk around thinking about a problem or question I have I'm in a kind of tunnel vision mode, not really seeing the sights around me. As soon as we started the Street Wisdom exercises, I was looking keenly at all the lovely and interesting things I was walking by.' Doug, San Francisco, USA

'An incredible tool and important movement, whether for personal exploration or to encourage creativity in business.' David D'Souza, London, UK

'Multi-day leadership trails in beautiful and remote locations are great for reconnecting with yourself. However, the nature of the street allows for that same magic. The session was the best-reviewed item of our Google Summer Fest!' Marcel, Amsterdam, Netherlands

'It was amazing to observe how a seemingly strange exercise turned out to be the most beautiful learning for our Sudarshan leadership team.' Ashish, Pune, India

'Your session was so much more than we expected – Street Wisdom contributed not only to the formation of plans for next steps in Lush's training but also to real connections between the group and a noticeable "recharging" of individuals. Thank you.' Katie, Poole, UK

You can read more tales from the street at streetwisdom.org.

Thanks

This book wouldn't exist without Street Wisdom, and Street Wisdom wouldn't exist without Mel, Mark, Rachel and Vanessa. Day after day you've been the people who've actually made the magic happen. And thank you, Sue, for keeping a wanderer like me on the straight and narrow (or at least trying to).

Thanks to my co-founder Chris Baréz-Brown (if it weren't for you and those mojitos…) and Chris Sollett for being there from the start. To Darius Norell for partnering on the Invisible University and to Esperide Ananas Ametista for helping the stars align on a moonlit Italian mountainside.

We wouldn't have made it through the early days without the enthusiasm of Street Wisdom champions like Mark Hall at the RSA, Scott 'The Boom' Morrison, Louise Cox Chester of Mindfulness at Work, our psychologist in residence Nikita Mikhailov and David Micklem, who wisely encouraged me to 'stick with it' and is now stuck with being our social venture's (very able) chairman.

This book has been a real pleasure to write. And that couldn't have happened without Vanessa Barlow, who has been my writing shadow every step of the way, nor without the patience and expertise of Xander and the team at Unbound.

I want to thank Jo, my wife and life-strolling partner, who somehow helped me find space to write while birthing her own career as a ceramic sculptor. My daughter, Elsa, has several times thrown herself into leading Street Wisdom events even when she felt out of her depth, but she and my son, Zachary, really get mentioned here in this roll of thanks because they are a wonder to me, every single day.

A deep bow (and a hug) to all who agreed to play the role of 'strangers' in the book and share some wisdom with us. They are (in order of appearance) Patrycja Slawuta, Lord Andrew Stone, Sir Ken Robinson, Suzy Walker, Gib Bulloch, John Lydon, Esperide Ananas Ametista, Nikita Mikhailov, Bruce Daisley and Charles Handy. And thanks to everyone who has contributed thoughts, words, ideas and goodwill to this book, including Jim Garrison and Peter Merry of Ubiquity University, Carl Honoré, Giuseppe Boscherini, Tim Stonor, Marc Mertens, Sara Hope, Mark Buckle, Edvard Olsen, David D'Souza, Atef Alshehri, Jem Lloyd-Williams, Fleur Carter, Andrew Furman, Lianne Campbell and Jyotish Patel. A thankful 'woof' to Arnold Mindell for shamanic inspiration behind the human compass practise.

Other Street Wisdom 'family members' I'd like to acknowledge include our Poet-at-Large, Philip Cowell (thank you so much for the opening poem), Nick Hammond for always having an eye on new opportunities, Izabela Dobrowolska for bringing more young people to Street Wisdom and all of our wizards who are out there leading events and making new discoveries. They include Sarah Storm, Bryony Farey, Anja Mutic, Andrew Paine, Claudia Monteiro, Justine Clement, Inés Alonso, Kev Wyke, Millie Baker, Jane Parslow, Susanne Taylor, Joyce Matthews, Kathryn Parkes, Jez Lewis and Karen Ward.

With thanks to Pete at Leagas Delaney for the cover design. And to Tim Delaney for creative counsel.

I want to send extra-planetary appreciation to two people who are no longer with us but whose influence I feel every day: Mark Adams (indelible Mark), whose infectious enthusiasm convinced me to set up our school for street wizards, and the unforgettably beautiful, natural phenomenon that was Sille Lundquist, who planted the Street Wisdom seed in Scandinavia. And while we are off-planet, I'd just like to acknowledge my 'astral flying instructor', David McCready. Never a dull moment with you on my wing, DM.

My thanks to the organisations who have partnered with us so far. They include The Royal Society of Arts, Creative Social, Made by Many, Seeds of Peace, Impact Hub, School of Communication Arts (SCA2), Curiosity Inc and Mindfulness at Work. Zul and SRLV – every social venture should have accountants like you. And very special thanks to Suzy and those lovely folk at *Psychologies* magazine for sponsoring our World Wide Wander as it grows every year.

To end where we began, I want to salute all of the people out there who have participated in a Street Wisdom event somewhere in the world – and to the volunteers who've led those events. You're the reason we do what we do and the stories you send back from all parts of the globe are the fuel we run on. I have been inspired by your tales and the wonders you've uncovered on your quests and have tried to weave what we are learning from you into what I have written here. Our shared journey together has touched, surprised, moved, delighted and inspired me. This book is my way of saying thank you.

Meet the Strangers

Patrycja Slawuta – MindHacker and founder of Self Hackathon. Page 27.

Lord Stone of Blackheath (Andrew) – Mindfulness Campaigner and peace activist. Page 57.

Sir Ken Robinson – Creativity Champion and educational disruptor. Page 86.

Suzy Walker – Editor and luminary of *Psychologies Magazine*. Page 114.

Gib Bulloch – Corporate Insurgent and intrapreneur. Page 145.

John Lydon – Advisor and client counsellor to Australasia's business leaders. Page 169.

Esperide Ananas Ametista – Consciousness Explorer and expert in intentional living. Page 191.

Nikita Mikhailov – Business Psychologist and Chief Neuroticism Officer. Page 215.

Bruce Daisley – Leading Podcaster and VP for Twitter Europe. Page 239.

Charles Handy – Social Philosopher, friend and (though he would never admit it) National Treasure. Page 257.

Index

Unbound is the world's first crowdfunding publisher, established in 2011.

We believe that wonderful things can happen when you clear a path for people who share a passion. That's why we've built a platform that brings together readers and authors to crowdfund books they believe in – and give fresh ideas that don't fit the traditional mould the chance they deserve.

This book is in your hands because readers made it possible. Everyone who pledged their support is listed at the front of the book and below. Join them by visiting unbound.com and supporting a book today.

Sergio Castro
Justine Clement
Rachel Crowther
Nat Delaney
Izabela Dobrowolska
Rhiannon Evans
Kameleon
Melanie Knight
Anja Lampert
Laurette Long
Chris Marks-Billson
Mark Morfett
Justin Mullins
Carlo Navato
Elizabeth Newton
Jonathan Pearl
Julian Roberts
Ian Sanders
Tim Scott
David Slight
Lorraine Spring -Taylor
Julia Wardhaugh